D0396320

Dr. Peeling's Principles of Management

PRACTICAL ADVICE FOR THE FRONT-LINE MANAGER

NIC PEELING

DORSET HOUSE PUBLISHING
353 WEST 12TH STREET
NEW YORK, NEW YORK 10014

Library of Congress Cataloging-in-Publication Data

Peeling, Nic
    Dr. Peeling's principles of management : practical advice for the front-line manager / Nic Peeling.
        p. cm.
    Includes bibliographical references and index.
    ISBN 0-932633-54-4
        1. Management. I. Title: Principles of management. II. Title.

HD31 .D679 2003
658.4--dc21

                                                                    2002041217

Cover and interior illustrations: Andrew Sellick
Cover design: Nuno Andrade

Distributed in the English language in Singapore, the Philippines, and Southeast Asia by Alkem Company (S) Pte. Ltd., Singapore; in the English language in India, Bangladesh, Sri Lanka, Nepal, and Mauritius by Prism Books Pvt., Ltd., Bangalore, India; and in the English language in Japan by Toppan Co., Ltd., Tokyo, Japan.

Printed in the United States of America

Library of Congress Catalog Number: 2002041217

ISBN: 0-932633-54-4   12   11   10   9   8   7   6   5   4   3   2   1

Dr. Peeling's Principles of Management

PRACTICAL ADVICE FOR THE
FRONT-LINE MANAGER

Also Available from DORSET HOUSE

Are Your Lights On?: How to Figure Out What the Problem Really Is
by Donald C. Gause and Gerald M. Weinberg
ISBN: 0-932633-16-1   Copyright ©1990   176 pages, softcover

Communication Gaps and How to Close Them
by Naomi Karten
ISBN: 0-932633-53-6   Copyright ©2002   376 pages, softcover

An Introduction to General Systems Thinking: Silver Anniversary Edition
by Gerald M. Weinberg
ISBN: 0-932633-49-8   Copyright ©2001   304 pages, softcover

Managing Expectations:
Working with People Who Want More, Better, Faster, Sooner, NOW!
by Naomi Karten   foreword by Gerald M. Weinberg
ISBN: 0-932633-27-7   Copyright ©1994   240 pages, softcover

More Secrets of Consulting: The Consultant's Tool Kit
by Gerald M. Weinberg
ISBN: 0-932633-52-8   Copyright ©2002   216 pages, softcover

Peopleware: Productive Projects and Teams, 2nd ed.
by Tom DeMarco and Timothy Lister
ISBN: 0-932633-43-9   Copyright ©1999   264 pages, softcover

Project Retrospectives: A Handbook for Team Reviews
by Norman L. Kerth, foreword by Gerald M. Weinberg
ISBN: 0-932633-44-7   Copyright ©2001   288 pages, softcover

The Secrets of Consulting: A Guide to Giving and Getting Advice Successfully
by Gerald M. Weinberg   foreword by Virginia Satir
ISBN: 0-932633-01-3   Copyright ©1985   248 pages, softcover

Find Out More about These and Other DH Books:
Contact us to request a Book & Video Catalog and a free issue of *The Dorset House Quarterly,* or to confirm price and shipping information.

DORSET HOUSE PUBLISHING CO., INC.
353 West 12th Street   New York, NY 10014   USA
1-800-DH-BOOKS   (1-800-342-6657)   212-620-4053   fax: 212-727-1044
info@dorsethouse.com   http://www.dorsethouse.com

Dedication

To Sue, Harriet, Jilly, and Sally

Acknowledgments

First, I would like to thank my employer, QinetiQ, for allowing me the use of work facilities to write this book. *Dr. Peeling's Principles of Management* was written in two passes: a first draft, which I wrote before I had signed with any publisher; and a major rewrite, which I completed based on advice from my editors at Dorset House Publishing and with a lot of input from colleagues, friends, and family.

There are many who deserve my acknowledgment for their help in shaping this book. First off, I am indebted to Neil Hepworth, who read each chapter of the initial draft as it was written and who gave me much encouragement and sound advice throughout the draft's creation.

I was most fortunate in having many friends and colleagues in addition to Neil who read the first draft and gave me feedback on it, including Mark Gamble, Cath Hipwood, Ken and Christine Magowan, Steve Mitchell, Michael O'Mahony, Eric Peeling, Thomas Petford, Sally and David Rees, Rob Rowlingson, Julian Satchell, Jutta Spaniol, Mike Wild, Arthur Williams, and Harriet Yeoman. For their line-by-line critiques, I am particularly indebted to Richard Chisnall, Duncan Machray, Betty Mackman, Matthew Peck, Anne-Marie Rocca, and Alan Watson.

Over the years, I have had so many conversations with friends and colleagues about the subject matter of this book that it is impossible to name them all individually; you know who you are and please accept my thanks. Some of you must be named, however: For your help in getting my thoughts straight for the second draft, I am particularly grateful to Gill Bates, David Hutchinson, Steve Mitchell, Julian Satchell, and Richard Taylor. For detailed comments on the rewrite, my appreciation goes to Richard Chisnall, David Hutchinson, James Kirby, Duncan Parkes, Matthew Peck, David Rees, and Anne-Marie Rocca.

I would like to conclude with some very special thanks. The staff at Dorset House Publishing has been incredibly supportive throughout the writing, editing, and production of this book. Along with the author Tim Lister, Dorset House has made a very significant creative and stylistic contribution to this work. Thanks particularly to Nuno Andrade, Vincent Au, Wendy Eakin, and David McClintock. I am also indebted to two colleagues, Andy Sellick and Andrew (Ed) Edmondson, for producing the amazing illustrations. Andy, Ed, and I worked up the ideas for the illustrations and Andy created all the artwork. As someone who has almost no artistic talent, I have found it a pure delight to work with such a professional and talented illustrator. My thanks to all.

Contents

3 Managing People in Teams: Leadership Principles 59

4 Managing the Practice of Team Leadership 80

CONTENTS

Introduction

Does the world need another management book? My conviction that it does—and that it especially needs *this* management book—and my enthusiasm for writing the book you hold in your hands developed as a result of my experiences when I first found myself in a management role. Like many others before and after me, I was quite good at my job (as a research scientist), and so I got promoted to be a manager of research scientists. Despite being given no training to help me prepare for my new role, I soon found myself in charge of a staff of fifteen research scientists who looked to me for management and leadership. From the start, I faced a multitude of problems that I felt sure had been faced by thousands of managers before me, and for which I suspected there must be a wealth of tried-and-tested solutions from which to choose.

Still most comfortable in my role as a research scientist, I went in search of books to read that would explain the basic theory and practice of management. My first stop was a good local bookshop, where I found a dozen shelves full of management books. Scanning the shelves quickly, I discovered management books on hundreds of fascinating topics: Some were aimed at students in MBA programs; others concentrated on a particular management theory, such as total quality assurance or reengineering; some were written by the growing number of management gurus; still others were anecdotal accounts from industry luminaries. A surprising number of books were aimed either at students or at top executives within an organization. What I did not find were books that encapsulated best practice for someone facing management responsibilities for the first time. By the time I found such a book, I was well into my management career and had learned enough to know that I did not agree with much of what it contained.

Having come to the conclusion that the book I needed as a front-line manager did not exist, I became enthused with the idea of writing one. In preparing this book, I have applied my training as a research scientist to the task: Much of what I have written has been influenced by existing work on management theory and is based on the theories that underpin management, such as psychology. However, I have not set out to write a scholarly tome; I believe passionately that there is a lot to be said about the subject of management and leadership that can be described straightforwardly, in black-and-white, unambiguous terms.

I have tried to codify in this book how to manage and lead well. I am sure you have experienced the effects of bad management, and that you know instantly when your management does something that is de-motivating, crass, or apparently stupid. Nevertheless, some things often taken for granted are improved by explanation. Accordingly, where I have explained the reasons behind the techniques, I do so because I hope you will find those reasons interesting and informative. However, the best test of the techniques is to apply them and see if they work for you.

WHO SHOULD READ THIS BOOK?

I believe that the most important levels of management in an organization are the top and the bottom. There are lots of books for chief executives, but I've found no good books for those who manage the workers directly responsible for creating the real value within an organization. This book targets those front-line managers within medium and large organizations, but a lot of what I describe will apply to small companies as well. The sorts of people for whom I wrote this book might think of themselves as team leaders or section leaders, but it is most specifically for someone undertaking such a job for the first time. More experienced managers should enjoy reading it to compare how much of my analysis of good practice agrees with their own.

STRUCTURE OF THE BOOK

The book follows my own journey through management, telling the reader the sorts of things I wish I had known when I started. It is divided into chapters that treat the following broad topics:

Managing People as Individuals: You've started Day One as a manager and you meet your first staff problem. You realize that making the wrong decision could cause someone real pain, a thought that should scare you. In this chapter, I describe the techniques that will encourage members of your staff to respect and trust you as their manager. I also describe many of the basic techniques of management, such as setting salaries, staff appraisals, recruitment, and the like.

Managing Problem Staff and Staff Problems: As you gain experience at managing people, you realize that there are a host of difficult problems to be addressed that you would really rather not face—misconduct, under-performing staff, harassment, and so on. This chapter tackles these problems head-on, and so must you!

Managing People in Teams—Leadership Principles: The awful realization dawns on you that you are not just a "manager." Your team is looking to you for answers, for direction, for inspiration. The chapter explains the fundamental qualities of a great leader, of which the top four are vision, determination, judgment, and integrity.

Managing the Practice of Team Leadership: As you come to see the qualities that a good leader should possess, you realize you do not possess them all. How can you lead your team in spite of your weaknesses? This chapter looks at techniques for leading in the real world, such as leadership style, delegation, banking credibility with your team, and my most radical suggestion—faking integrity.

Project Management: You realize that you are expected to serve as the leader of a team within the hierarchy of your organization. In this chapter, I analyze how team management differs from project management.

Managing Different Types of Staff: You discover that you must manage both the different personalities and behavior patterns of different professions. Without intending to perpetuate stereotypes, in this chapter I discuss lawyers, IT staff, creative types, consultants, salespeople, and support staff.

Managing Team Culture: You realize that to be successful as a team leader, you need to foster a strong team culture. Some teams have great team spirit and obviously share the same values and aspirations, as is shown in the sections of this chapter, which describe how to build a strong team culture.

Managing a Failing Team: You are about to face the greatest challenge a manager can face: turning around a failing team. The sections in this chapter describe how to accomplish this glamorous but distinctly challenging task.

Organizing Your Team (and Yourself): Your team is growing, the pressures on you are building, and you start to realize how difficult it is to delegate tasks properly. The chapter treats the topic in a straightforward and practical fashion.

Managing Your Universe: As your team starts to deliver the goods, others in your organization begin to see your team as a threat. There is a constant stream of initiatives from your own organization that seem to be designed to keep your team from doing its job. Increasingly, you must act as the interface between your team and the rest of the organization—without losing your temper. The chapter focuses on ways to handle this role.

Managing People Outside Your Organization: It is clear to you that no team operates as an island. How you must learn to deal with your customers, suppliers, partners, and people from different cultures is treated in this chapter.

Revisiting Common Management Themes: You've mastered a lot of what it takes to be a good front-line manager but there are some remaining topics that every new manager will encounter. To address these issues, I include a chapter that summarizes common management themes.

Managing in the Real World: In this chapter, I present some practical examples, which describe various problem scenarios, and I give my ideas on how to handle each.

Drawing Conclusions: The brief final chapter contains some remarks about why I think being a manager is the best job in the world.

LITERAL-READING WARNING

I assume that you, the reader, are a busy person. I want you to read this book, so I have kept it fairly short and have tried to express my ideas in a colorful and memorable style. However, there are potential problems in the style that I have used:

- *You may take me too literally.* In places, I have exaggerated or simplified points to help them hit home. My aim is to help you think about the issues, not to produce a recipe that can be followed precisely. Every management job has its own unique context, and this book must be interpreted sensibly in the context within which you work.

- *You may think you understand a point, and then not know what action to take in a real-life situation because I have made what to do seem more straightforward than it really is.* The theory of management is simple; it's the practice of management that's hard and that cannot be learned fully from a book. What I have tried to do in this book is provide a framework for you to use as you think about your job and as you master the practice of management. To help you move from theory to practice, I make lots of suggestions for techniques that you might like to try, but remember, they must be adapted to your context.

THE GOLDEN RULE OF MANAGEMENT

The single most important principle that new, front-line managers will do well to keep in mind is what I call the Golden Rule of Management:

> *You will be judged by your actions, not by your words, and your actions shall set the example for your team to follow.*

The truth and the implications of this rule will be apparent time and again in numerous forms, not only throughout this book but throughout your future as a front-line manager.

The Cast of Characters

Edgar

66 Hi, I'm Edgar, a successful and expert manager. You see me pictured here with four members of my team. I'm the one smiling, in the middle. In order to facilitate a multi-stage process of communication and understanding of the principles described throughout the book, we will be on hand to illustrate key do's and don'ts—well, mostly the don'ts—of management. Seeing us on a page should help you crystallize your understanding into a thorough and proactive knowledge mass. At the end of this experience, I'm confident you will feel as empowered, valued, energized, and set to take on the world as my team does at the end of each and every day. 99

Dr. Peeling's Principles of Management

PRACTICAL ADVICE FOR THE FRONT-LINE MANAGER

CHAPTER 1

Managing People as Individuals

The challenge of managing people well and my desire to share my ideas on how to manage people better were what motivated me to write this book in the first place. Let's face it: Throughout the world, the standard for managing people is pretty dismal. Most people remain motivated to do their work in spite of their managers' efforts, not because of them.

Why is the standard so low? I believe the primary reason is that new managers do not understand the basic principles behind managing people. By examining and explaining those principles, I hope to make the process of managing much less daunting.

PRINCIPLES OF MANAGING PEOPLE

One of the problems that people have as new managers is that they do not understand that the principles of people-management are little different from the principles of being a good parent or a good teacher, namely that they must

- set high expectations of people's performance and behavior.
- set clear boundaries for acceptable behavior.
- impose discipline and, where necessary, punishment when behavior is unacceptable.

- set clear boundaries of acceptable performance and then work with under-performers to improve performance. If performance cannot be improved, decide whether the under-performer needs to leave the project or, in the worst-case scenario, whether he or she needs to leave the organization.
- provide clear, immediate feedback, praising good performance and constructively criticizing poor performance, to show what is required.
- set an example personally of the expected performance and behavior.
- behave in a way that wins respect.

Being a parent or teacher is a great responsibility. Managers have to accept that they are doing a job with similar levels of responsibility to those of parent or teacher. As a manager, you may find this role a bit uncomfortable, but your staff will have no trouble at all accepting that this is the way good managers should behave.

In writing the last item in the list above—*behave in a way that wins respect*—I was struck by the overlap between the problems that face the people-manager, and the problems that face a leader. Managing people and leading people both require that you have the respect of the individual members of the team. Many of the qualities of the manager and leader are the same. They include honesty, courage, decisiveness, integrity, acceptance of responsibility, and consistency. But there are additional qualities that you need in the people-management role. They include fairness, empathy, caring, protectiveness, and approachability.

Before looking at specific aspects related to managing people, let's look at some of the key attributes that a good people-manager must have: first, the respect and trust of the staff, and second, good communication with the team.

RESPECT AND TRUST

An issue that has always troubled me is whether management is a form of *manipulation*. I would really like to believe that you can be a manager without being manipulative, but it is my opinion that managers have no other option at times. The uncomfortable truth is that when resolving all the different pressures from existing customers, your own organization, bids for new business, and the like, you are inevitably going to have to persuade people to do things that are not entirely in their own interests. It is also an uncomfortable truth that you are not always going to be in a position where you can explain the bigger picture to your staff. All that you can hope to achieve is a level of moral manipulation—that is, to find a situation such as the following:

If your team knew the whole picture, the majority of members would support your actions.

One of the reasons that staff members may not trust a manager is that they know that managers sometimes must have divided loyalties. Managers of teams are truly caught between a rock and a hard place. On the one hand, you as manager will probably be loyal to the team; indeed, you probably like to think you are part of the team. On the other hand, you are a representative of management, albeit possibly the most junior, and so the team will correctly suspect that you are one of "them," and not really one of "us."

Balancing what is best for the organization against the best interests of my team's members is an aspect of management that gives me many sleepless nights. As manager, you must decide in each case where to draw the line. This is an unquestionably difficult task, but I do have a piece of advice:

Members of your team should know exactly where you and they stand.

5

In other words, a decision that clearly favors either management's or the team's best interest—but not both—is not an issue to fudge. When you have listened and discussed the issue with each person concerned, then you need to tell the whole team what your decision is, and why you have made it. You have to make it clear that your decision is final and that people have to accept it. Too often, I see managers fudging the unpopular decisions, or blaming senior management.

A corollary of this wisdom is

As manager, you cannot be an ordinary member of the team.

Just because you will have to make hard, unpopular decisions does not mean that you are an uncaring person. Going back to the analogy between management and parenting, good parents can say no to their children frequently, while maintaining a loving, caring relationship with them.

One of the reasons for mentioning the issues of manipulation and divided loyalties is that many managers complain that their staff members are suspicious of their motives. It basically comes down to whether your staff respects and trusts you. Staff suspicion is quite natural and you can only create the necessary levels of trust and respect by your openness, honesty, and integrity.

How open should you be?

A good starting point is to be as open and honest as possible. What the clause "as possible" means in practice, however, is difficult to define. I tackle this issue by listing the circumstances in which I believe less-than-total openness can be justified:

- *The effort of communication is not worthwhile.* You will never have as much time as you would like to have to communicate with your team. The sad truth is that even if you spent every minute of every day communicating, that would not be enough for some people. You have to view communication as an investment in a healthy team, and decide what level of investment you think you can afford. This means you have to prioritize your communication, and consequently, some issues will drop off the bottom of the list.

* *You need to respect confidentiality.* You may be instructed by your organization to keep certain information confidential, or you may not be able to release information that was told to you by someone in confidence.
* *Full disclosure will unnecessarily disrupt or distract your team.* A good example of information sometimes better withheld might be the latest initiatives from headquarters. Many of these never actually get implemented in a way that is as threatening as they first appear. My approach to such issues is to openly answer any questions about them. I try to go occasionally to group gatherings, at coffee break for example, so that people can quiz me. In this way, I make it clear that there is no secret about what is going on, but I also demonstrate that I am relaxed about such things and imply that if and when they impinge on the team, I will immediately brief everyone.
* *Full openness would cause unnecessary pain.* On occasion, you may need to discuss how a member of your team can improve his or her performance. You may decide to be selective in describing specific failings in order to help the individual handle and respond positively to your criticism.

Openness is the underpinning property of all communication. In the following section, I discuss the topic of interpersonal communication with *individual* team members. In a later chapter, I discuss the issue of communication within the context of leadership of your team.

COMMUNICATION

Managers often proclaim, "I always have an open door," but, for many staff members, this exhortation has become pretty meaningless. A much more positive message to give your staff members is, "You must come and tell me about any problems you have, and I will not be happy if I find you have been bottling things up."

To back this up, of course, you will have to make yourself accessible. This approach can only work if you provide people with plenty of opportunities to talk to you and if you always make people's need to talk a top priority. Saying, "Come in and sit down" is more positive than reaching for your appointment book to arrange a time to talk at some point in the future.

Communicating with your staff
requires that you listen.

Communicating with your staff requires that you listen, not just talk. Listening is a skill that most people must constantly work at to do well, but there are a number of techniques that can help you become a better listener:

- *Eliminate avoidable interruptions.* Divert your telephones, beepers, pagers, and the like, so that they do not require your response. If you have an office with a door, post a "do not disturb" sign or ask someone to intercept visitors. If you work in open plan, find some other, more private place where you can meet without distraction.

- *Tell the person if you have a time limit.* If you can meet only for a specific length of time because of some other commitment, tell the person in advance and then stop worrying about scheduling conflicts. By being open about your commitments, you can then give the person your undivided attention during the time you meet.

- *Ask open questions.* You will learn more relevant information if you ask questions that cannot be answered by a simple yes or no. For example, ask, "Why do you think you have difficulty talking to John about this?"

- *Do not finish other people's sentences or talk before they are finished speaking.* To listen well, you have to go at the other person's pace. If you need to hurry things, do it tactfully, taking care not to interrupt mid-speech.

- *Act interested, even if it is an act.* Sometimes, by feigning interest even when you don't feel genuinely interested, you will find that you become more involved in the issue under discussion. At the very least, don't look bored.

Act interested, even if it is an act.

- *Don't be judgmental or argumentative.* People will nearly always react negatively if they feel they are being judged or blamed, whether fairly or unfairly. Use factual phrasing that removes any tone of accusation, saying, for example, "I was upset" rather than "You upset me." Encourage people to learn from their own mistakes by talking openly and uncritically when problems arise. If you behave otherwise, your staff members will avoid taking risks and will not tell you when they have made mistakes.
- *Think about how the other person perceives things.* People often correctly accuse their managers of not understanding their point of view, and not appreciating the problems they face in trying to do a good job. Make every effort to avoid being that kind of manager.
- *Don't jump to conclusions.* Keep an open mind, and let your staff know that you want to hear all the facts.
- *Treat people as individuals.*

The last point is extremely important—so important in fact that I've separated out my reasons from the bulleted list to expand upon them as follows: Good people-management is predicated on getting the best out of people. This means that you have to know what motivates an individual, and also what upsets him or her. You need to understand an individual's strengths and weaknesses. The only way to do this is to talk with each person on your team so that you know what makes the individual tick. One-on-one conversations build strong relationships; strong relationships build the team. However, in your role as manager, you must be wary of crossing the line between relationship-building conversations and interference.

When does healthy interest become an invasion of privacy?

In some instances, a manager's interest in a staff member's activities can be interpreted as prying or worse. To avoid problems, I warn new front-line managers that an invasion of privacy occurs *whenever the person involved thinks it does.* When I am the manager, I bring this issue up explicitly, emphasizing that people must tell me directly—and immediately—if I have broached a subject they find uncomfortable. You, like me, most probably are not a trained mental-health professional or counselor and, while listening to someone seldom does harm and often helps, offering advice on personal issues can be dangerous and almost always should be avoided. Restrict your discussions to how you can help the individual handle the business implications of any issues that verge on the personal.

When does your healthy interest become an invasion of privacy?

How dearly people hold their privacy is evidenced by the fact that most people will only talk to you if they trust you—as a person and as a manager—so you need to avoid doing things that will destroy that trust. Certain behaviors are sure to damage a trusting relationship, as detailed below:

Be wary of repeating confidences to your bosses. If you repeat confidences inappropriately, your behavior is likely to kill any trust your team has in you. Of course, there are times when sharing a subordinate's confidences with your management will be necessary, but repeating confidences to an untrustworthy boss is an invitation to disaster for you as a manager. When you find yourself in a situation in which passing on a confidence to your boss seems in your team's best interest, let your decision to speak or remain silent be influenced by the degree of trust you have in your boss to respond in the way that you want. Keep silent until you are sure the repeated confidence will be respected.

Do not gossip about confidences. Never tell anecdotes about things you discovered in confidence—even if you believe you have made such anecdotes anonymous. The person whose confidences are featured in an anecdotal exchange will feel humiliated and resentful—not feelings that are conducive to trust between manager and staff.

Do not tell the same thing differently to different people. If your team suspects that you take a different line with different people, their trust in you will evaporate.

Don't say things about people that you wouldn't tell them to their face. To behave one way behind a person's back and another in direct encounters with that person shows a deep lack of moral fiber on your part. Never allow yourself to sink so low.

Do tell the truth and be straightforward with people. Immediately following four negative admonitions, this last affirmative seems obvious and easy to follow. Don't be fooled: Being honest and straightforward can be difficult. In my consideration of whether management is manipulation, I discussed this issue and pointed out that you will not always be in a position where you can explain the true situation to your staff. The important thing to remember here is that a manager always should try to be as truthful and straightforward as possible.

PEOPLE-ORIENTED ROLES AND DUTIES

The various people-related tasks a front-line manager must handle can be daunting. Some managers view certain people-related tasks as real horrors—setting salary levels and preparing staff performance reviews and appraisals, for example—but I will start this section by looking at the part of my job that possibly gives me the most pleasure: staff development.

Staff Development

In my opinion, the most important principle to keep in mind during staff development can be expressed as

The right job, for the right person, at the right time.

Allocating people to the right jobs seems to me to be the key to developing staff. When a new job provides an appropriate challenge to someone, that person can then suddenly improve in his or her capability. Regrettably, a typical approach to allocating staff can be summed up by "I have a job that needs doing. Natasha is free—she can do it."

Or, putting it another way, "I have a square hole. I have a round peg. Pass me a hammer."

The problem with doing it properly is that you make a lot more work for yourself, as the following dialogue illustrates: "I have a square hole. The square pegs are already in use, so I'll move the most appropriate square peg. One of my triangular pegs could grow to fit that newly available square hole, but every triangular peg is currently in use. . . ."

Given that "growing" a staff member's capabilities is largely achieved by finding the right job to challenge the individual at the appropriate time, you must understand the particular strengths of each member of your team, and choose jobs for each that capitalize on those strengths. I am surprised and dismayed by how often people are deployed on jobs that do not play to their strengths. Indeed, it often seems to be an unspoken organizational policy to give people jobs that play to their weaknesses, in the mistaken belief that this will help them strengthen one of their weak areas.

I think that a manager should encourage people to volunteer for jobs. If someone is doing a job he or she wants to do, that person will often go the extra nine yards to make a success of it. But how do you persuade someone to do a dull or unpleasant job, one for which no one is likely to volunteer? There is nothing wrong with judicious bribery, saying, for example, "If you complete this job on time, I will give you a bonus of five hundred dollars." There is also nothing wrong with leaving a light on at the end of the tunnel. People will often do an unpleasant job provided they know it is for a fixed duration, after which they will have an opportunity to do something more to their liking.

Because staff development is so linked to what jobs a person does, people tend to develop at an uneven rate. It is well worth letting staff members know that this uneven rate of development and advancement in the job is entirely normal, and that they should not get worried if their career coasts for an extended period. You will find that even the best workers usually have had prolonged periods when their careers did not progress quickly.

I wish I could speak more positively about the role that training courses can play in developing staff, but my experience has been that they are of limited value. On the other hand, I have found that using an experienced person to mentor someone less experienced while the latter tackles a new task can be very effective.

I also wish I could be more enthusiastic about formal career-development plans that try to structure an individual's professional development. Again speaking from my own experience, these formal plans generate far too little value for the time they consume. The trouble I see with them is that after a career-development plan has been agreed to by an individual and a manager, it not uncommon to find that neither of them will look at the plan again until the next career-development meeting. To provide any significant value, the formal process must be an ongoing commitment by both management and staff. There will be contexts in which this is worthwhile—with young recruits, or when someone is recovering from a period of low productivity, for example—but most of the time, I find little to justify the effort expended.

Staff Reviews

Although I have serious doubts about the value of formal career-development plans, I am convinced of the need to regularly review staff performance. Your organization may mandate annual appraisals, but even if it does not, you should review the performance of individual staff members at least once a year. I tend to perform such appraisals in preparation for salary reviews. There are a number of different aspects that can be included in an appraisal, but I think there is one consideration that dominates all others:

Are there some aspects of a person's performance that you feel he or she should improve?

If there is some way that an individual can become more valuable to the organization, he or she is entitled to be told about it. It sounds obvious, but time and again I see managers failing in this duty.

In an appraisal, I try to give the person being reviewed a thumbnail sketch of what I consider to be his or her strengths and weaknesses. I look back over the past year's performance and state what I believe the person did particularly well. I describe any areas where my expectations were not met. I then discuss with the person whether my assessment is fair—it is very important to find out whether we both have the same perceptions. Finally, I ask the individual to describe specific aspirations for the future, for example, what challenges would particularly excite him or her. At the end of the discussion, we will decide together whether any particular action needs to be taken to improve the individual's performance or enjoyment of work.

Determining Salaries

My first observation about setting pay is a comment on human nature itself:

> *Staff members will be affected first by how their salaries compare with those of other team members, second by comparison with others in the organization, and last by comparison with others outside the organization.*

This means that getting the pay differentials right within the team should be your highest priority. Of course, pay is just one dimension of an organization's reward structure, so you actually should concentrate on getting the *reward* differentials right within the team. Unfortunately, because people tend to compare each individual element of their reward structure, you must ensure that each part of the structure is fair: You have to get pay differentials right, make promotion decisions correctly, implement bonuses and other incentives fairly, and so on.

Even if you work in an organization that tries to keep the details of people's pay in the strictest confidence, I recommend that you assume that most members of your team will have some idea of what others are paid.

The process I recommend for establishing staff salaries consists of four steps.

First, talk to each member of your team about his or her desired salary. This discussion with each person on your staff will alert you to those people whose aspirations need to be moderated. Although some people may ask for the moon, you will probably be pleasantly surprised at how modest many people's aspirations are. If you are taking over as manager of a previously assembled team, these discussions will allow you to find out whether promises regarding salaries were made to people by their previous manager. Information about promised salary increases is particularly important because people naturally feel indignant when they believe promises have been broken. You do not have to match a salary level committed to by your predecessor, but you will want to discuss your decision with any individual who feels financially disadvantaged now that you are manager.

Second, work out your overall salary budget and then sit down with a list of staff members, noting the "ideal" salary you would like to pay each. To calculate "ideal" salaries—that is, the salary you would pay a particular person doing a particular job if money (and related rewards considerations) were no object—you will need access, if possible, to the pay levels of staff outside your team, and also some idea of what your people would be paid by your competitors. It has been my experience that pay levels advertised in the press tend to be higher than the average levels paid in the engineering and software industries, but you will want to confirm what is the true situation for your field and locale. Your Personnel or Human Resources (HR) department should be able to provide you with up-to-date figures, but if not, you will have to do your own research.

Following this process will help you set the right relativities within your team.

Third, try to get everyone's salary as near to the "ideal" pay as your organization can sanction. If you are not given complete autonomy to set pay levels for your team, then it may be time to brush up on your political skills. Having done your homework as you prepared your list of ideal salaries, you will find it easier to argue for your people.

Personally, I think it is worth telling team members the process and any applicable formula you and the organization use to set pay levels. If you do not share this information with your team, then people may suspect that you are holding out on them or even worse.

Last, let people know individually what their approved salary or pay raise is before they get official notification. By communicating specific details to each person about the salary or pay raise he or she will receive, you can soften the blow for those who will not get their hoped-for remuneration. It will also maximize the beneficial effects when someone gets more than he or she expected.

The process I am recommending is time-consuming, but pay is so seldom a motivator and so often a powerful de-motivator that I think you have little choice but to find the time.

A common misconception about pay is that it is simply a reward for good performance. It is more complex than that—what a person is paid should be appropriate to the value of the person to the organization. What this really means is that pay *is* a reward for good performance but is further determined by the person's value to the larger organization. If you wish to use money as a reward for your staff, then consider some form of one-time bonus, not an increase in salary.

Although most employees might wish to dissuade a manager from believing the following, you can seriously damage someone's career by paying him or her too much. Eventually, someone who is overpaid is likely to disappoint the employer, and ultimately may face humiliation and other forms of grief. Such people may even end up losing their job because their salary exceeds their value to the organization. People typically adapt their life-style to their salary—those who are overpaid may face significant hardship if they eventually have to take a job with a more appropriate salary.

My final points about pay relate to two well-researched but surprising statistics:

1. For professionals, such as computer programmers, the difference in productivity between the best and worst performers is typically 10:1.[1] In my personal experience, this is an *under*estimate, because there are many jobs that the best performers can do that lesser performers would fail to finish.

---

[1] For more on productivity, see Frederick P. Brooks, Jr., *The Mythical Man-Month* (Reading, Mass.: Addison-Wesley, 1975), and Tom DeMarco and Timothy Lister, *Peopleware: Productive Projects and Teams*, 2nd ed. (New York: Dorset House Publishing, 1999).

2. The difference in salary between outstanding employees and average employees in the United States is just 3 percent.[2]

I may not win many popularity contests with the following idea but I do suggest you try to beat the 3-percent differential, both by rewarding the better performers with bonuses, larger salaries, and plum assignments, and by offering below-average performers infrequent or no pay increases. Despite my recommendation, you may find it surprisingly difficult to hold back the pay of below-average performers. Your organization may even make it hard for you to do this, but I think it is worth the fight. If you are told that you will make matters worse by demotivating such staff members, please keep in mind that it is my view that such workers are seldom very motivated, so you will do little harm. On the contrary, by clearly showing that you do not think their performance matches their salary, you increase the chance that they either will improve their productivity dramatically or will voluntarily leave the organization. You will also improve the morale of the better performing staff members who will see that they get a proper differential for the extra value they deliver to your organization.

One issue that will make staff members particularly twitchy is if they suspect that you pay people based on how they look, act, and talk, rather than on what value they actually deliver to the team. You need to make it clear that you reward achievement and effort, not appearance.

Promotion

Many larger organizations have an explicit stratification that reflects a person's status. Smaller organizations may have a similar stratification system even if it is informal. Whether the

---

[2] The 3-percent differential is explained in Craig Eric Schneier, "Capitalizing on Performance Management, Recognition, and Rewards Systems," *Compensation and Benefits Review* (Mar-Apr 1989).

organization is large or small, however, promotion from one level to the next can have an equal, if not greater, effect on morale as pay does. Promoting the wrong people will seriously undermine the team's trust in your judgment, as well as demoralize your staff.

Before making a final decision about any proposed promotion, run through your plan with a few people whose judgment you most trust in the team. The greatest danger is that you will promote someone who looks more qualified to you than he or she does to peers and subordinates. Another danger in acting without feedback from judicious team members is that you may promote people because they have worked on projects that particularly interest *you*. Because promotions are visible to all and are exceedingly important to both those who get them and those who are overlooked, you cannot be too careful in awarding them.

Recruitment

Earlier in this chapter, I observed that the general standard of people-management is dismal. In truth, *dismal* is far too kind a word to describe most recruitment procedures.

Some organizations centralize recruitment, making the hiring of new staff the responsibility of the Personnel or HR department. If your organization takes this approach to hiring, I suggest you try to get permission to screen the recruits who are targeted for your team *prior to their being hired*. Another possible approach is to front-load the selection process either by posting job announcements on appropriate Internet sites or by placing job descriptions at career offices of local schools and colleges. There generally is no fee associated with either of these approaches, enabling you to place essentially free advertisements. Any promising candidates can then be passed on to your organization's centralized process, accompanied by your request that the recruits, if successful, be sent to your team. If that does not work, then be creative and find some wiggle room to get involved in the selection of the recruits—it is that important.

Assuming you can select your own staff, I offer the following advice that has worked well for me in interviewing and hiring professional analysts, consultants, programmers, and research-and-development (R&D) staff:

- Identify and document the precise qualities and skills required for each open position, and then ensure that your recruitment process tests candidates for those qualities and skills. (Doing this will increase the chances of selecting the right candidates, and also provides protection against potential claims of discrimination.)
- Ideally, you should devote a full day's time to the selection process. (If a whole day seems like a lot of time, you may want to spread the recommended seven-to-ten hours over two or three days. I urge you to take the full amount of time, however, as the investment is well justified, especially when weighed against the cost of hiring the wrong person. My personal observation is that, in general, spending more than a day does not significantly increase the chance of making the right recruitment decisions.)
- Conduct the interviews in your normal working environment, making sure to expose the candidates to the team culture and the team to the candidates.
- Use the formal portion of the interview to bring out each candidate's personal qualities. (In the formal session, I do not look for professional or technical expertise, but rather try to see who the person is: introvert or extrovert? leader or follower? externally motivated or self-motivated? accepting or judgmental? highly ethical or relaxed standards? There is no right set of personal qualities, but only a right match with the team and job. A good way to uncover personal qualities is to ask candidates to illustrate their answers by giving examples

from their own experience, perhaps saying, "Can you give me an example of a recent situation in which you used your leadership skills?")

- Use the informal portion of the interview to probe each candidate's professional expertise and experience.
- Ask candidates to bring examples of their work with them to the interview, but also give them a written test as part of the interview. (Whatever the skill required, an on-site test should be mandatory. I have too many times seen programmers hired by organizations that have not reviewed even one line of code written by the person, but I have also seen programmers who supplied as their own creation samples of code actually written by someone else. The on-site test assures that in hiring, you'll be safe, not sorry.)
- Ask each candidate to prepare a ten-minute presentation describing some experience of personal interest. Follow each presentation by having a small group from your team spend ten-to-fifteen minutes asking the candidate questions on the presentation topic.
- Give each candidate a short, practical test that focuses on the skills and abilities required to do the job. (I typically allow about thirty minutes for the test, and choose a brief case study in which the candidate must analyze a fairly general, work-related problem.)
- Schedule an informal, one-on-one session with the candidate and a new team member, so that the candidate can determine what the work environment is really like.

Undoubtedly, you will think of additional questions and tests that suit your environment and culture, but the suggestions given above provide a starting point. One sometimes-difficult point to remember is: Try to handle the process as informally as possible. Not only do you want to find out about the recruit, but you also want the recruit to decide whether he or she likes your team. There is no reason the experience cannot be enjoyable for the recruit and for you and your team. If the process is fun, the candidate you've decided you want is much more likely to accept your job offer.

After the selection process has been completed, I usually gather everyone who has taken part. Then, I ask people to share their views on the candidates' qualities. This group gathering has a number of advantages: It is informative; it helps get the team to buy in to new members; and it shows that I value the team's opinions. In the end, the final decision is mine, as manager, and I must be committed to accepting full responsibility for any mistakes, but input from the group is highly important to the process.

Because the world I see around me seems increasingly litigious, I recommend documenting each stage of the recruitment process and keeping written records for both accepted and rejected candidates. A well-run and well-documented recruitment process should provide a solid defense against any potential claims of discrimination.

Do's and Don'ts

I believe that every front-line manager needs a stockpile of good techniques to employ as needed and a working knowledge of common pitfalls to avoid. The remainder of this first chapter provides a discussion of both.

Give others the credit and take the blame yourself. When it comes to taking credit and accepting blame, I abide by a very simple rule:

The team gets all the credit; the manager gets all the blame.

If the team you manage screws up, you can criticize your own staff, but do not allow your superiors to criticize your team directly—your managers can shout at you, not at your team.

Put your staff first. The easiest way for your staff members to know that they come first is for you to put them first. When an urgent staff problem comes up, do you do everything

23

humanly possible to deal with it right away? The Golden Rule of Management discussed at the end of the Introduction suggests that if a front-line manager does not try to drop everything to handle staff issues, then people on his or her team will know where they come in the manager's list of priorities—and it's not number one.

When you make a mistake, apologize. When was the last time your boss apologized to you? When did you last apologize to your staff? An apology, genuinely offered, will usually be accepted. When people know that they can apologize when they make a mistake, they—and you—will probably notice a reduction in the level of stress and an increase in people's willingness to take risks. Both behaviors are positive for a team.

Manners maketh managers. Can anyone tell me why so many managers seem to ignore the demands of common courtesy? What your mother taught you about saying "please" and "thank you" applies just as much to the workplace as it does to your social and family life. Remember to praise staff members who have done a job well. The Golden Rule of Management also tells you that by being courteous yourself, you'll assure that courtesy will become an integral part of the team culture.

Be aware of your emotional state. The Golden Rule of Management means that your emotional state can infect your staff very quickly. For example, if you are depressed, it will be easy to depress your people. If you lose your temper, the effect on your team can be severe (although, paradoxically, an occasional outburst can have a positive effect because it may demonstrate how strongly you believe in something). If you are upset because of some event in your personal life, it will be all too easy for people to be worried that something bad is happening at work.

There are two possible ways to deal with this problem. First, you can guard against displaying your emotions when you know that your emotional state is not normal. Second, you can be open with people about the cause of your emotional state by saying something like "please forgive my somber mood; I have a family problem on my mind" or "I'm sorry if I'm a bit irritable but I didn't sleep well last night" or "please excuse me if I seem distracted but I think I may be getting a migraine."

Beware of events that arouse strong emotions in your staff. People react with strong emotions when dealing with issues about territory, status, unfair treatment, and blame. You need to tread very carefully when any of these situations arise. For example, don't expect a reorganization of offices or desks to go smoothly and not take up a lot of your time.

Beware of showing signs of status. Managerial perks such as a large, plush office or a reserved parking space tend to put barriers between the team and yourself. I believe that doing away with such status symbols helps team building.

Keep your promises to your staff. On the surface, it seems obvious that you must keep your promises to staff members, but let me state it even more strongly: *Do not make promises you cannot keep.* When committing to something, keep in mind how busy you are, and avoid the temptation to offer things unless you are sure that you will have the time and the resources needed to deliver them. Few promises are broken deliberately or because a manager could not deliver; they are broken because the person making the promise was *too busy* to deliver. The best solution is not to have made the promise in the first place.

Do not trust the wrong people. I know it is not very helpful to read advice stating that a manager must be careful not to trust the wrong people—how do you know which individuals to trust? In my experience, there are two ways to determine trustworthiness. First, you can train yourself to be a good judge of character; second, you can see which team members are most respected by the rest of the team. The first approach may or may not come easily to you but the second method only requires sufficient contact with the team and competent observational skills. I recommend the second method. One of the most common traps new managers fall into is to develop a close and trusting relationship with someone the team does not respect.

Do not show favoritism toward individual staff members.
Showing favoritism is a very common mistake for managers to make. It is all too easy for you to give out signals that tell the team which staff members are "in favor" and which are "out of favor." This is a particular danger when you strongly like or dislike a staff member. You will need to make a conscious effort not to favor people you like, or to treat people you dislike less well than they deserve.

Avoid giving any staff member an unpleasant surprise. If you have to do something that a staff member is not going to like, try to ensure that it does not come out of the blue. As discussed previously, tell staff members in advance what the outcome of a pay review is likely to be before they receive formal notification. Equally important, if you are going to formally warn a member of the team about under-performance, make sure he or she knows well in advance that you have some performance concerns. Staff members can easily, and justifiably, feel aggrieved if unpleasant things happen to them without any warning.

Conduct exit interviews. One of the problems managers have is that they do not really know how they are perceived, or how various team members view the team as a whole. One way to learn how people on the team regard you and the rest of the team is to talk informally in an exit interview with anyone who leaves the team. If you make it clear that you really want to know how people perceive you, the team, and your organization, many exiting employees will give you a frank insider's view. If the person is leaving under unhappy circumstances, you may get a tainted picture, but often you will be able to identify underlying issues that you may want to correct for the future.

Avoid inconsistent behavior. Behavior that can be interpreted as inconsistent can greatly undermine your authority in the eyes of your team. In numerous places in this book, I advocate that you take hard, and at times ruthless, action. To establish yourself as being "hard but fair," apply the Golden Rule of Management and be as hard, if not harder, on yourself as you are on others. Ensure that you are consistent, and hence even-handed, in your treatment of your staff.

Manage people according to the accepted norms of their job. Different types of jobs have different norms for what is considered acceptable behavior. Following such norms should not be interpreted as being inconsistent. Rather, behaving in accordance with the norm for a particular job is the correct action to take. In a later chapter in this book, I observe that salespeople sometimes behave in a way that would be completely unacceptable in other staff—for example, by embellishing product claims. Similarly, certain behavior that would be tolerated in a team setting—for example, extreme eccentricity—would be totally unacceptable if it occurred in front of a customer. A third example of how different jobs have different acceptable norms of behavior appears in the next chapter, where I discuss why a front-line manager might treat key staff members differently from other staff. As manager, you will not lose respect by recognizing that different jobs are judged by different standards, provided you are consistent within each category of job, but you may have to make it *explicit* that you have different rules for different types of people. Knowing how and when to apply this management paradox is an essential skill for the front-line manager.

Never set unrealistic deadlines. I go somewhat ballistic when I come across deadlines that are impossible to meet. I am even opposed to *stretch* deadlines—those deadlines that are so tight that they have no contingency to accommodate a slip here and a slide there. Such research as I have read regarding deadlines in the computer software field tends to back up my own observation that tight deadlines de-motivate, and unrealistic deadlines completely de-motivate. Research indicates that even *self-imposed* tight deadlines de-motivate. If this observation strikes you as fallacious, I suggest you try an experiment: Set an unreasonably tight deadline for yourself on a task you must complete and see what emotions bubble to the surface.

Be wary of workaholics. Many people take their work and their careers very seriously indeed. Generally, this is a very positive trait, but there can be a downside when such people become so driven that they work excessively long hours and take very little vacation. As a consequence, their judgment can become flawed, they can make too many costly mistakes, and they can become unproductive—the very opposite of what they have set out to achieve. As a front-line manager, it is one of your most challenging jobs to pull such people out of the downward spiral of workaholism.

Avoid excessive multi-tasking. When pressures on a project build, new front-line managers may find themselves faced with the temptation to overload staff—and especially key staff members—with too many jobs. There is a lot of truth in the saying that "if you want a job done quickly, then ask a busy person to do it." However, there comes a point when people have so many disparate responsibilities that they cannot focus adequately on any of them.

Choose the team's targets and incentives very carefully. Targets and incentives do motivate particular forms of behavior, and well-chosen targets and incentives can work extremely effectively. However, do not be surprised if your team responds to every target and incentive you set, to the single-minded exclusion of everything else. Some managers seem to love setting lots of targets, and offering numerous incentives, as a means of motivating staff. You, however, should remember that targets and incentives are a very crude mechanism that often leads to behavior and practices that are not in the team's long-term best interest.

I can illustrate this danger with a simple example: A sales-person who is compensated in relation to the *volume* of business booked is unlikely to push very hard for the best possible price. In such a situation, if you expect to preserve your margins, you must establish incentives that link bonuses to product *price.* For more on this topic, see Chapter 6.

Never pretend you know more than you do. Some managers hate admitting they do not know something. Your team will respect you much more if you freely admit your ignorance and ask to be informed. Asking questions—even when you suspect they may seem stupid—is a sure sign that you are not stupid. *Do not tolerate office politics within the team.* Office politics—and the ambitious, small-minded people who play political games on the job—can quickly undermine team spirit. I suggest you stamp hard on the first sign of politics infecting your team. Staff members who are playing political games do not behave in an open or straightforward way, so be forewarned: If you cannot determine the motivation behind someone's actions, office politics may be at work.

Give trust before it has been earned. Your staff members will not grow in their jobs until they have made the mistakes that all inexperienced workers must make for themselves. You should be tolerant of these mistakes—unless, of course, people are making the same mistakes over and over again. As manager, you will need to give trust to staff members who have not yet earned that trust, because if you do not, they will never grow to become fully productive workers.

Overreact when the situation calls for it. It is all too easy to underestimate the speed and intensity with which you need to react to staff problems. It is fairly obvious that issues such as harassment, discrimination, and health and safety violations require strong and rapid responses. It is less obvious that problems associated with under-performance, staff morale, and staff retention can accelerate into becoming big problems very rapidly indeed. Provided you do not overreact to everything (thereby giving the impression of panic), overreacting seldom does harm, but underreacting can have very serious consequences.

Know when to administer benign neglect. In the previous paragraph, I noted the possibility that you will have to react very quickly to certain problems. Surprisingly, the opposite technique can also be useful. In certain circumstances—for example, when people are becoming overly emotional—it can make sense to move slowly. Managers tend to be action-oriented people, and it can be quite difficult for them to just leave a problem alone, and let nature take its course. Knowing when to act and when to hold back is probably best learned through experience as, unfortunately, there is no magic test to distinguish problems that need a rapid response from those that will benefit from benign neglect.

Avoid management-speak. Many people feel alienated by the jargon of that obscure dialect of English called *management-speak*—a form of communication that relies on words such as empowerment, human resources, competencies, envisioning, reengineering, total quality, and so on. Avoid using terms that emphasize that you are the manager and that the listener is your subordinate—staff members will have greater respect for you if your actions rather than your words show your authority. Although lesser-known than management-speak, the dialects of *vision-speak* and *mission-speak* should be avoided as well. By using plain English, you will offer people a refreshing change.

While I'm on the topic, I also recommend you avoid management clichés. "We are a listening organization," "My door is always open," "You are empowered to . . . ," and the greatest lie of all, "People are our greatest asset," are management clichés that should be avoided like . . . well, like the plague.

Avoid management-speak.

Show people it's okay to have fun. Managing your staff is much easier if you can inject some informality and humor into your relationship with your team members. Show people that it's okay for them to have fun in their interactions with you, and also in their interactions with each other. As a front-line manager with many responsibilities and pressures, you may need to consciously make yourself relax a bit. (As a stiff-upper-lipped Brit, I know what I am talking about.) But whether you must consciously force yourself to relax or you are one of the lucky few for whom relaxing comes easily, it is important for you to try.

Showing team members it is okay to have fun is one aspect of your job as manager—associated with this is the need to ensure that neither you nor members of your team behave in such a way as to take all the fun out of work. So many work environments are high-pressured and so many managers feel overworked and stressed that it is hard to remember there is more to work than showing up and collecting a paycheck. By loosening up a bit, you and your team members can still enjoy the tasks and challenges you each liked when first starting out in the field.

Draw the line between work and home. There is no universally accepted place to draw the line to separate your work from your home life. I often see people allowing the demands of work to cut deeper and deeper into the time they should be devoting to their families and social activities. This behavior is not good practice for managers or for team members, and so I encourage you to draw a solid line between work and home and then stick to it.

It is very possible that you will draw your own line in a place that some team members will find uncomfortable. Because of the Golden Rule of Management, people on your team will probably interpret your line as the line you want everyone to adopt. This should not be encouraged, and so you must make it very clear that team members need to draw their own lines, and that within reason, you will respect their decisions and not undermine them by pressuring anyone to work excessive overtime. Eliminating long hours or overtime is easier said than done: One of the less desirable features of a strong culture is that it can coerce people to do things they are not comfortable with. A long-hours culture is a common example of this effect, one that I have seen far too often.

SUMMARY

The principles that underpin good people-management are little different from those that apply to good parenting:

- Set high expectations for performance and behavior.
- Set clear boundaries for unacceptable performance and behavior.
- Confront poor performance and behavior.
- Provide immediate feedback on both desired and unacceptable performance and behavior.
- Impose discipline if behavior remains unacceptable.
- Set a good example with your own behavior.

The point about setting a good example with your own behavior is particularly important and another example of the Golden Rule of Management. You can only manage people well if they respect you, and no one will respect managers whose actions are not principled.

The other key point to remember is that a successful people-manager has to be a good communicator. Even if you are not naturally a good communicator, you must make the effort to talk to your staff, and perhaps more importantly, *to listen to your staff*.

Finally, one concept is discussed in the chapter that all front-line managers should adopt as their creed:

Always treat people as individuals.

CHAPTER 2

Managing Problem Staff and Staff Problems

The preceding chapter was quite optimistic in that it described many situations in which a manager's actions can benefit the staff he or she manages. You may find this chapter somewhat difficult because it addresses many of the issues that give kind-hearted managers sleepless nights—misconduct, under-performance, termination, personal problems, harassment, and the like. Be forewarned, but please take a deep breath and read on, because it is the handling of these hard problems that separates the average manager from the great manager.

HANDLING THREE TYPES OF STAFF

Typically, three types of employees are likely to take up a considerable amount of your time. Knowing how best to manage them is a good investment for any level of manager, but it is especially valuable for the front-line manager. The first category consists of key staff; the second, under-performing staff; and the last, low-value, high-maintenance staff.

Handling Key Staff

Conventional wisdom dictates that managers should handle key staff differently from the rest of the team. You, as a front-line manager, need to know both *why* this is true and *how* key staff should be managed. In the previous chapter, I stressed that you must never tell different people the same thing in different ways—however, you will want to understand when to handle different people differently. Innate feelings of fairness may lead you to espouse "equal treatment for all" and to fear accusations of favoritism, but there are several instances in which different treatment is justified:

- Key staff members often possess superstar qualities, contributing phenomenal skill, energy, and talent to your team, but there can be a negative side to those qualities—such as with the superstar who designs brilliant software but can only work under the pressure of a final deadline, at night, during overtime hours. It is reasonable for you to invest a high percentage of your management time to managing these negative aspects. In my own world of research scientists, there is a common saying that "the line between genius and insanity is often blurred." This is a complete lie. *A line? What line?*

- Key staff members usually know their value to you and to the greater organization, and may be tempted to try to use their position to their advantage. Anyone else trying this trick is very easy to deal with, but key staff members may require special handling. It does make sense for you to spend a greater portion of your time establishing yourself as their manager, making it clear to all that the positions of manager and staff have not been reversed. It is also worth keeping in mind that some key staff members may be so valuable to the organization that if they go above you and complain to your boss, your boss may back them, not you. Gain the trust and respect of key staff early on so as to avoid embarrassment or irreconcilable differences in the future.

One important issue to decide is how far you are willing to go to keep key staff members happy. The following suggestions can help:

Do not pretend that you are not dependent on your key staff. I have seen managers try to downplay the value of their most important people. While it is certainly true that no one is indispensable, do not deprecate the value of key staff members. Acknowledge the important role they play as individuals and as team members. Acknowledge as well the role that others play, helping key people to see themselves as part of a team, not as superstars.

Maintain a dialogue—not a monologue—with key staff members. Many people leave their job as the result of some small issue that becomes the straw that breaks the camel's back. By keeping close contact with all members of your staff, you should be able to spot the "straws" before anyone nears the breaking point. Because people usually drop hints about grievances, your well-cultivated dialogue channel will help you detect problems. Sorting problems as soon as they arise is much easier and cheaper than handling them after a situation has become a crisis.

It may seem obvious that you must know who your key staff members are. However, it bears repeating that they are not just the flashy superstars. Key personnel may also include quiet workers who are vital to keeping your business alive. You would not discriminate against someone because of race, religion, creed, or nationality—do not discriminate against someone who is quiet!

Know who your key staff members are.

Respect individuality. People who strive for excellence in performing their jobs are often strongly individualistic. The converse is also true: A staff member who has a strong, confident personality and who is outspoken about his or her preferences tends to excel on the job. A good rule to apply to managing all staff members is to show respect for people's individuality, but this rule is especially important when managing the top-notch staff members you really do not wish to lose. When key staff members feel that they are expected to conform to behavioral norms set by their organization or their team, they usually rise up in some form of revolt—a situation every front-line manager wants to avoid.

As a front-line manager, you must guard against giving the impression that you would be happier with a team of well-behaved company clones than with a team whose key staff members require special handling. As manager, you need to make it clear that you value diversity, and that you will tolerate individuality and eccentricity, as long as a person's behavior is not harmful to anyone.

Establish a good team culture as the best protection against prima dons and donnas. If people among your key staff value the respect of their teammates, they will not want to lose that respect by being overly demanding. A gentle statement such as "I am worried about how that will look to the rest of the team" can sometimes work wonders.

Ensure that key staff members are having enough fun. It is all too easy for new, front-line managers to load key staff members with important but unexciting jobs, to the extent that they end up getting little pleasure out of their work. Find out what motivates key staffers and make sure that the mix of tasks you assign them enables them to enjoy their work. Happy people, engaged in tasks that challenge and absorb them, are much less likely to leave your team than people who conclude that their professional likes and dislikes are inconsequential to you.

Do not yield to threats. On occasion, you will need to decide how far you are willing to go to retain key staff members. Once you have established your upper limit, then be consistent in sticking with it. Most organizations cannot or will not pay a salary or provide a benefits package that matches what a poacher will offer, but you need to know what package you can counter with as best-offer. It is my view, however, that you should not respond to someone's threat to leave by matching the poaching salary. To do so is likely to cause such dissent among other key staff members that the situation will quickly get out of hand. Your best strategy is to find out why the person is considering leaving, and hope that by addressing that essential issue, you can convince the employee to stay. You might also propose changing the employee's duties if new challenges would increase job satisfaction enough to keep him or her on board.

If it appears probable that you will lose a key staff member, bringing in your boss to talk to the person can be productive. Your boss's commitment to keeping the person in the organization will flatter the person, but the meeting may also allow your boss to determine whether other challenges in the organization might convince the person to stay, or whether the person might be relocated to a position that might justify a larger salary or better benefits than you can offer.

Do some "succession planning." I am not a great advocate of planning for all contingencies, but it is worth working out how you will handle the situation if a key staff member leaves, particularly if he or she is putting pressure on you either to exceed your upper limit or to change duties in ways that will not benefit the team. Although I do recommend investing lots of effort in keeping your key staff members happy, it is important to know when it is time to let someone go.

When you lose a key member of the team, do it with grace. It is good business to make every reasonable effort to keep a valuable employee on your staff, but if the departure is inevitable, be gracious. It is surprising how often your paths are likely to cross again. It is conceivable that the employee, at some future point, may even want to have his or her old job back. It is just as possible that you may move to a new company and discover yourself supervising your former employee once again. Keep in mind that there is almost no situation in which you can benefit from someone leaving your team on bad terms with you.

Handling Under-Performing Staff

The second type of staff member to require a disproportionate portion of a manager's time is the under-performer. Make no mistake about it: As manager, *you must tell staff members if they are under-performing.* My advice may seem obvious, but many managers do not face up to this task. Nevertheless, a manager who always tackles under-performance and misconduct issues head on usually reduces the stress level among staff members. Make it clear that no news is good news—that is, if you don't tell people that they're under-performing, it means that you are satisfied with their effort.

When disciplining (or firing) someone for sustained under-performance, do it "by the book." How should you handle someone who is under-performing? Much of this section describes how to help someone overcome performance problems, but you, as a front-line manager, must keep in mind that the problems experienced with some under-performers could get to a stage where formal proceedings will need to be initiated. Handling this very serious situation is especially difficult because different countries have different laws designed to protect employees from being unfairly dismissed. You need to know what constitutes unfair dismissal in your locale. Different organizations also have different processes for handling under-performing staff. Rather than attempt to describe the laws of one country or another, I recommend that you find out exactly what your company's procedures are and follow them to the letter. If your organization has an established Personnel or HR department, staff within it probably will be able to offer you support and advice. There are times to do things by the book, and this is one of them.

Identify the cause of the problem. When determining whether to take punitive action, make certain that you can answer yes to the first question that follows and no to the second: First, is the staff member aware that he or she is not performing adequately? Second, is there an underlying problem that is causing the under-performance? You need to ensure that both of you have the same understanding of the problem before you can decide how best to address that problem.

When supplying criticism, you must not accuse or blame the person. The reason for pointing out a person's failings is that increased awareness can help the person address the problems caused by those failings. By taking this approach, you constructively criticize behavior; you are not blaming the person. As you probably already know, if you blame people for their failings, they are unlikely to listen to even constructive criticism. You may even know this firsthand: If you believe that your managers will blame you for failure, then you may be tempted to try to cover things up, and will avoid taking risks. The people you manage will exhibit the same reaction, so make sure you do not create a blaming culture within your team. Remember: A blaming culture happens by default; if you do not actively fight against it, then a blaming culture is what you will get.

When supplying criticism,
you must not accuse or blame the person.

Set achievable, measurable targets for improvement. It is important that under-performing staff members know precisely what is expected of them. Targets must be sensibly challenging and their achievement easy to measure.

Do not bear a grudge. After an under-performing staff member has been disciplined or has been given constructive criticism, both you and the staff member may feel uncomfortable in dealing with each other. You must set the tone by dealing with the person as if nothing negative has happened. If the person shows resentment and sulks, then you need to decide whether it's best to ignore the apparent ill will (for a while at least) or whether you should have a quiet conversation with the staff member to reinforce the fact that you are trying to help him or her recognize a problem and learn from it.

Recognize that a person's failings are often the flip side of a strength. We've all seen situations in which someone's weakest trait has a highly desirable flip side to which it is inextricably tied. For example, someone who displays irritation and impatience around slow-paced colleagues may possess great personal drive and take pride in accomplishing superhuman tasks. In such circumstances, you, as manager, should acknowledge both the positive and negative attributes, reinforcing what is commendable and suggesting that the negative behavior be recognized and controlled by the individual. Be realistic about how much improvement can be expected, however. Few people can totally overcome their failings.

Sometimes, you will discover that under-performance is a result of the person doing a job that does not play to his or her strengths; in which case, a change of job may provide the best way to solve the problem.

Never undermine a person's self-respect. Respect is key to a healthy team. To expect team members to show both respect for self and respect for each other is not an unreasonable requirement. People who are not performing adequately in their current job on your team should be shown the same respect that key staff members are shown. Most probably, the job is a poor match with the person's qualifications, but under-performance in one job does not mean that the individual would not blossom if assigned to a different job, a different team, or a different organization.

Be consistent in how patient you will be with under-performers, and beyond that, act ruthlessly. Employees need to know that they have a reasonable amount of time to address problems. They also need to know you will properly analyze the reasons for under-performance and address those causes, even if the result of the analysis means a job relocation, a change of supervisor, or some other remedy. However, your team cannot carry passengers indefinitely: Under-performers are a potential threat to the survival of the team. In addition, it is not kind to leave a person struggling—most everyone wants to do a good job, so the under-performer is probably unhappy with his or her work. Once you have decided that the person has been given sufficient time to improve, you need to decide, with appropriate consultation with your superiors and the Personnel or HR department, whether the person is redeployed or fired.

As manager, I tend to be considerably less understanding with someone who repeatedly makes the same kind of mistake than with someone who makes mistakes when attempting a new task. I rapidly lose patience with the repeat offender and often conclude that the person is not worth retaining as my employee.

Use any probationary period to weed out under-performers. It is astonishing how many under-performers are identified as such during a probationary period, but manage to make it through onto the permanent staff. In many countries, and in many organizations, it is vastly easier to dismiss a person on probation than it is to dismiss a fully ensconced under-performer.

Many managers worry about how teammates will react to firm management action against under-performers. It has been my experience that, provided you allow a reasonable time for improvement, most team members would be more ruthless than you are—after all, they have to carry the under-performing passengers.

Handling Low-Value, High-Maintenance Staff

As discussed above, key staff members often require a significant investment of your time, but in most cases, you will willingly invest this time because they contribute great value to your business. Under-performing staff members also deserve a disproportionate percentage of your time to help them improve until such time as they become less needy or you determine they require too much overhead to justify keeping them on the staff.

In an ideal world, the above two categories of employee would require the majority of your time and the remaining staff members would go about their business without much intervention from you. However, in the real world of the frontline manager, there are likely to be other people who are of only marginal value to the business but who also require a sizable chunk of time. These are staff members who constantly moan about the way you and your organization treat them. These are people who think they are much better than they really are, and who will never understand why their talents are not appreciated to the degree they expect. These are people whose personalities cause them to fan the discontent of others. From your own experience as a team member and now as a new manager, you can probably add plenty of other types of personality to this list. The question then is: How do you best deal with such staff?

The best solution to this problem is to avoid it in the first place. Try to identify such individuals during your recruitment process and do not hire them. If you spot a difficult employee during a probationary period and cannot cure the problem, then fail the probation.

No matter how hard you try, at some point or other, you will encounter problem staff members who are not absolutely crucial to your business but who are on the team because they perform some necessary role. When this happens, you will want to try two steps to remedy the situation. First, determine whether the problem can be solved, even partially, by making the individual aware of why the behavior is unacceptable in your view. If the problem can be solved in this way, then this is the place to start. There will, however, be staff members whose fundamental personality traits mean they will be a constant problem for you. An example of this sort of person is the staff member who has too high an opinion of himself or herself and expects to be treated better than is merited. Do not waste too much effort on such people, as they and you will be better served by moving them off the team.

The second step to take to attempt to remedy the situation involves honestly assessing whether the person lacks value because he or she is in the wrong job. Could such a person's value be increased by a change of duties, either within your team or elsewhere in the organization?

If you are faced with a situation in which there is no apparent solution, what can you do about high-maintenance, low-value staff members? I recommend you calculate whether they are worth the management effort. If not, then you can be ruthless about rationing the amount of time you spend on them, or you can look for an opportunity to move them out of your team. In the case of staff members who imagine themselves to be better performers than they are, you can state honestly that you do not have as high an opinion, and suggest that they find a different environment in which they can reach their full potential. Whatever action you take, you need to stay within the legal constraints that govern constructive dismissal. If you find my approach too brutal, then you can carry your problem staff members and hope they eventually leave. This managerial approach is fine, provided that your problem staff members only cause you minor problems; if, however, they cause significant problems for you and the rest of your team, then I urge you to take appropriate steps.

It is very important that you not give in to this sort of person in order to keep the appearance of a properly functioning team. You must not give the problem staff member undeserved pay raises, and you must not give in to unreasonable demands. If you do, you will have earned the discontented reaction that you probably will get from the rest of your team.

Managing key staff members, under-performing staff members, and low-value, high-maintenance staff members may take a disproportionate amount of a manager's time, but one of the most stressful and onerous duties that a manager faces is that of handling misconduct.

HANDLING MISCONDUCT

It is likely that every reader of this book understands what constitutes misconduct, but in the context of the front-line manager's purview, misconduct most typically relates to unacceptable behavior such as poor timekeeping, dishonesty, or harassment. It is important to distinguish misconduct from under-performance. To be considered misconduct, the behavior at issue must clearly be the fault of the person, behavior that is within the person's control; hence, the person is to blame. In a case of under-performance, it should be assumed that every person wants to do a good job but, for whatever reasons, the under-performer cannot. Accordingly, under-performers are not to blame, and it is your role to help them improve their performance. Sounds simple, doesn't it? Unfortunately, misconduct is sometimes closer to under-performance than you might think. For example, if someone's marriage is breaking up and the person is stressed as a result, then poor timekeeping would be more forgivable than it would be if there were no such mitigating circumstances.

When handling a case of misconduct, the first thing you as manager should do is find out whether your organization has specific procedures for handling the particular type of misconduct. For example, many organizations take a very strong position on dishonesty and may move straight to dismissal if there is a clear case of even a minor infraction.

Even if no specific procedure is indicated, many companies issue general guidance on how to respond when an employee's honesty is in question. Recommended action might start with an interview in which you issue a verbal warning, to be followed by a written warning if needed, and, if the behavior does not cease, to end with some sort of punishment. Before you take action, talk to your Personnel or HR department for advice. Sharing your concern with professionally trained members of the Personnel or HR department has the added advantage that it gives them early warning of the problem, which, when documented, can be part of an important paper trail if matters turn nasty at a later date. Among the details you will need to determine is whether you need a witness when you interview the person. It is a sad comment on modern life that misconduct cases are an ever-growing cause of legal action; you need to manage that risk by obeying organizational and legal requirements *to the letter*.

Before issuing even a verbal warning to the person concerned, gather all relevant, factual information. You do not want to waste your time or that of your staff member disputing the facts of the case. Disputes about facts will undermine your ability to retain control of the interview.

Before you meet, make a list of all issues you want to cover during the interview. Also prepare a list of whatever actions you intend to take before the interview terminates. Putting these in writing will help you keep control of the interview.

Although your action must be guided by your Personnel or HR department's advice as well as by the specific laws of your community, I recommend keeping the following process in mind:

- Start with a clear, concise description of the alleged misconduct.
- Give the person a chance to address the allegations and to offer any explanations for his or her behavior. Based on what you are told, you may need to decide whether the information warrants further investigation or a

move to a less confrontational agenda. Remember, you can always suspend the interview at this point.

- Clearly and precisely, state what you expect the person to do. Generally, this course of action will be nonnegotiable and you should avoid getting sucked into negotiating details. Record details of the expected course of action in writing after the meeting and give a copy to the staff member.

- To conclude the interview, tell the person what will happen next, and what could happen beyond that.

Once you have concluded the interview, carefully record details of your conversation and the employee's responses, and note whatever further action is required of you. In addition, if there are specific dates by which you need to review progress or initiate further action, immediately record them in your calendar. Interviews of this nature can distract and distress new managers, but forcing yourself to keep accurate, factual records will help you keep focused and in control.

Firm, prompt action is enough to resolve a misconduct case in a vast number of situations. However, there remains the possibility that you may occasionally have to apply the ultimate sanction—termination.

TERMINATION

Imagine that the worst possible scenario has occurred and the employment of a member of your team must be terminated. How should you go about this unpleasant task?

The first thing I suggest to new managers is that unless you are instructed otherwise, you should conduct the termination interview yourself and not leave it to Personnel, HR, or anyone else. I believe it is important for your team to see that you have the courage to handle such situations personally. However, you may either want to, or be required by law or company policy, to have a second management representative present during the termination interview. The rationale behind this is simple: Both you and the employee may benefit from having a witness to the event.

Second, before you move to terminate employment for misconduct, verify that you have recorded facts properly *and that you have the documentation to prove that termination is warranted.* Confirm that all procedures for termination have been followed to the letter. If they have not, work out with Personnel or HR how you can best implement any procedures that were missed.

Although you should previously have thoroughly researched policy regarding termination, you will again want to talk to Personnel or HR professionals to double-check your organization's termination policy. In the hopefully rare cases in which you believe that the person being dismissed will have an extreme reaction, such as becoming irrational, violent, or vengeful, then you should coordinate your efforts with the Personnel or HR department to manage the risks.

The third matter to decide in advance of your meeting is what will happen after the termination interview has been concluded. In certain situations, you may require that the person first be met by someone from Security—either from an internal security department if your company has one or from an outside law enforcement agency if no other option exists—or by a specially trained HR staff member, and then be taken to clear his or her desk before being escorted off-site. In other situations, you may feel you can trust the person to do all this without an escort. Occasionally, the person may stay on to work out a period of notice. Each of these situations must be planned for prior to the final interview and then carried out as planned.

There are still other details to consider. For example, whenever the person will leave, whether under escort directly after the termination interview, later that same day under his or her own steam, or after a period of notice, you or a representative from the Personnel or HR department will need to collect company property from the employee's possession. Such items as the employee's keys, security badge, beeper, personal computer, or whatever may have been issued to the employee during the term of employment will need to be returned. Consider as well whether you'll need to disable computer-system access prior to the termination interview or after it. A very important bit of information to be covered in the termination interview concerns the employee's options for continuing insurance coverage, as applicable.

Think about whether the dismissed employee, if overly distraught, will be safe to drive home alone or whether you need to arrange for a taxi or for someone to drive? The planning you do prior to dismissing an employee shows the employee and your remaining staff that you are mindful of showing respect for the individual, despite issues of misconduct. Your concern for the human side must at all times be evident from your actions, whether during employment or termination.

I describe three steps for conducting a successful termination interview in the following section, but first review some key points:

Remain calm and business-like. If you have done things properly, the person being terminated should not be surprised. This does not mean that the person will not be shocked—he or she probably will be very shocked. The kindest thing you can do is to be calm and business-like, as this will help the individual to maintain his or her composure.

The person being terminated should not be surprised.

Keep the termination interview as short as possible. The meeting will be agony for the person being dismissed; prolonging the interview is cruel. *Avoid getting sucked into discussions or negotiations.* By this stage, the die is cast. You need to make it clear that an irrevocable decision has been made, and that the termination interview is essentially a one-way communication. You may well feel empathy for the person being fired, but you must avoid expressions of sympathy that open up the chance for prolonged discussion. *Be totally honest.* Any lack of honesty on your part is unfair and can get you and your organization into serious legal trouble.

The Termination Interview

A termination interview comprises three clear steps:

1. Inform the person than an irrevocable decision has been made to terminate employment.
2. Tell the person clearly and truthfully why employment is being terminated. Give the background, making it clear that the organization's procedures have been followed to the letter.
3. Describe the mechanics of termination and what will happen after the interview. Include information on how the individual will collect personal belongings; when he or she must leave; whether there is a severance package, and if so, what it will contain; whether you can provide a reference; what paperwork needs completing; how outstanding pay, if any, will be transferred; and any other details relevant to the particular situation or company.

Post-Termination Actions

Decide in advance of the termination interview how and when you will tell the team and any customers with whom the person had interactions, about the termination. You need to perform a difficult balancing act that combines honesty with an approach that does not taint the person's reputation. You must remember that you cannot be sure that the person who was terminated will not contact other team members and customers. Ensure that customers will continue to enjoy the same level of service, or better, from your team now that the person has left your organization. Be sure to convey this assurance of service before a disgruntled former employee can damage your relationship with a customer.

Although I hope you will need the advice in this section on termination very infrequently, you should be prepared for every eventuality.

STAFF PROBLEMS

A significant amount of your time as a people-manager can be taken up dealing with the effects of your staff's personal problems. Before discussing some specific problem areas, I offer the following general advice:

Remember that you are not a counselor. Listening to people's personal problems is fine. Discussing how to minimize the impact on their work is also fine. Offering advice on people's personal problems is beyond the bounds of what a manager should do.

Let the individual decide how much to tell you. You have no absolute right to know people's personal problems. However, if staff members want to tell you their problems, then you can help them manage the impact the problems have on their work. How much an employee tells you about personal problems is up to the employee—only the gentlest probing from you as manager is acceptable. If a person does not share details of a personal problem with you, then you will need to deal with any work effects without any additional knowledge—but you cannot excuse under-performance or misconduct just because you suspect that the behavior relates to someone's personal problem.

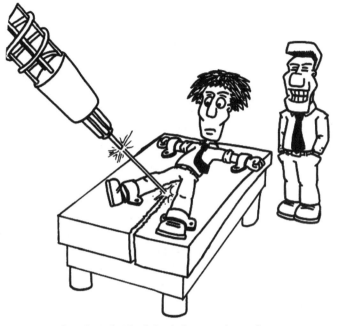

Let the individual decide how much to tell you.

Although there are many types of employee problems that a front-line manager may face, two areas are especially important to address: health problems and problems with alcohol or drug use.

Health

You need to broadly understand what effects people's health problems have on them. For example, if you think that a migraine is simply a bad headache or that someone should be able to overcome depression in a short period of time, then you are not going to manage staff with such problems very well.

How can you find out more about the employee's condition? First off, you can ask the person to explain what the effects of the condition are, and you can request literature that you can read. Second, you can research the employee's specific problem on the Internet, which has large amounts of information on nearly all medical conditions.

You have both a legal and a moral duty to manage members of your staff so that neither you nor the organization causes them physical or mental harm. Similarly, you have an obligation to be understanding, within reason, of physical or mental problems over which the individual has no control. If an employee's health problem suddenly flares up, you will need to discuss whether the employee can continue to perform his or her duties, or whether you can modify the duties or provide extra support in order to allow the individual to continue doing roughly the same job. Alternatively, you either will need to assign new duties within your team or will want to consult with your Personnel or HR department about transferring the person elsewhere in the organization.

One of the most difficult situations you can face is when you suspect that someone on your team shows symptoms of a mental health problem. One difficulty may be that the person involved may not recognize the need to seek medical help. If your organization has medical personnel on staff, then they can be approached for assistance in such circumstances. If no medical personnel are available for consultation, you still need to be proactive. It is my personal view that any indication of mental illness merits attention. Often, people silently suffering from mental problems will be helped by a manager's suggestion that they seek medical advice, as this will remove the onus from them to make the decision. It is never wise to encourage someone to "tough it out."

Alcohol and Drugs

Alcohol or illegal drug use only need concern you as a manager when the taking of such substances occurs during work hours, when usage has a detrimental effect on the staff member's ability to perform his or her work, or when usage threatens the user's or other people's safety. Someone who, in your opinion, drinks excessively in the evenings and at social events may concern you, but unless the person's performance at work is affected or his or her behavior at business-related social events is offensive, then it's not your business to intercede. When abusive drinking or illegal drug use—or both—take place during work hours, it is very much your business—as well as possibly being a matter of legal concern.

How do you positively identify alcohol or drug abuse in the workplace? There are signs that can help you confirm your suspicions. For example, you may be able to smell alcohol on a person's breath or see the effect it has on a person who appears to be inebriated. Drug use is more difficult to identify, but tell-tale signs may include

- mood swings, short temper, disorientation
- frequent visits to the rest room
- physical deterioration, runny nose
- deterioration in work performance
- increase in absenteeism
- increase in accidents
- relationship problems
- financial problems
- suspicious phone calls

If you are confident that your suspicions are correct, confer with your own management as well as with a Personnel or HR representative to determine the course of action. In most organizations, you as manager will be given the okay to talk to the person about your suspicions. If the person admits to the problem, you again will need to work with Personnel or HR to help him or her tackle the problem. My personal belief is that you as manager should be very tough and insist that there be no further alcohol or drug abuse at work. Make it clear that backsliding will not be tolerated.

If the employee denies that a substance-abuse problem exists, then you should describe relevant performance issues, tell the employee that you will note details of the discussion to be included in the personnel file, and that you will seek upper management's intervention if you continue to suspect a substance-abuse problem. Be forewarned that addicts who have not faced up to their addiction will have no compunction about lying to you and may quite possibly become a danger to themselves and others. You cannot in good conscience ignore such situations.

HARASSMENT AND DISCRIMINATION

Many countries have enacted stringent anti-harassment and anti-discrimination legislation that covers issues such as gender, race, and disability. Such legislation is extremely valuable from a human rights standpoint, but the downside is that in some countries, filing lawsuits that claim harassment or discrimination in the workplace has become a growth industry.

As a front-line manager, you must respond *by the book* to any harassment or discrimination allegations, whether made against you, against a member of your team, or made by any member of your team against you or anyone else. It is essential that you know your organization's policy, that you notify your management and the Personnel or HR department immediately as to the details of any allegation, and that you and others scrupulously follow procedures as mandated.

To diminish the chance that you might find yourself in a situation in which you could be accused of harassment or discrimination and to set a proper example for the rest of your staff, state your absolute conviction that comments or jokes about sensitive issues such as gender and race are completely unacceptable. Take your conviction one step further, however: Express your immediate disapproval upon hearing team members make inappropriate comments or jokes about sensitive issues.

Now go a step further: Verify that your support processes (recruitment, for example) do not discriminate against people on the grounds of sex, race, religion, national origin, age, or any area morally reprehensible to you or covered by your country's discrimination legislation.

Three issues that most front-line managers will face at some point in their careers are the general issue of how to handle harassment; the thorny issue of how to handle sexual relationships in the office; and the cerebral issue of how to handle your own unspoken thoughts, opinions, and prejudices.

Handling Harassment

I am really taking my life in my hands as a Protestant, Caucasian, heterosexual male, offering advice on how to handle harassment, but the following is based on my observations of how I have seen harassment issues handled successfully during a fairly long career in management.

Distinguish the sad from the bad. Most on-the-job harassment cases fall into one of two very distinct camps, which I label the *sad* and the *bad*. The *sad* situation is usually due to the inadequacies of the person doing the harassing. For example, if someone behaves in a way that seems sexually immature or inadequate, he or she can make members of the opposite sex feel very uncomfortable. Or, if someone comes from a culture or upbringing where intolerance was rife, that individual may well pick up intolerant speech patterns and habits. In neither of these cases is the harassing individual likely to be intentionally malicious.

The *bad* cases are those in which individuals use forms of harassment, such as sexual intimidation or bullying, to impose their will and power on others. In my view, being somewhat tolerant of the sad is not unreasonable, but being even the tiniest bit tolerant of the bad is unacceptable—the bad should be confronted and then stopped from continuing such destructive behavior.

There will be cases in which the person being harassed will find it difficult to know whether he or she should confront the person doing the harassing. For example, if a sad type of harasser is making life intolerable for someone, there may be no alternative but to confront the individual and stop the harassment. However, it is not as easy to determine the right action to take when the harassment might increase as a result of the confrontation. In general, it is probably worth confronting sad harassers because the majority of such people will respond positively to being confronted.

55

Confront harassment. What I am about to recommend may seem somewhat controversial: I believe that victims of harassment should lodge a formal complaint only as a last resort. I say this because I have observed that those who lodge complaints usually suffer greatly for their courage. The main problem someone who lodges a claim of harassment may face is the not-uncommon view that he or she should have been able to handle the situation without having to make a formal complaint. The most effective approach—one that seems to cause the least suffering on the part of the person being harassed—is for the harassed person to firmly and unemotionally confront the harasser on each and every occasion of harassment *and tell the person to stop.* Because bad harassment is usually about power and hatred, this approach gives the harasser the minimum amount of gratification.

As manager, you must confront harassment directed at individuals on your team whenever you have evidence that it exists. Have no doubt about it: When the boss tells someone to stop the harassment, the order is usually considerably more effective than when the victim of the harassment asks the harasser to desist. If nothing stops the bad behavior and you have to lodge a formal complaint of harassment on behalf of one of your staff members, you will be in less danger than the subject of the harassment would be if he or she were to make the complaint personally, because it will be seen that you are acting without any personal, emotional involvement.

Sex

No, I have not included this section because I have heard that sex sells books. I include it because there is a well-recognized connection between sex and power. As a manager, you have power over those on your team and there is a real danger that a sexual undertone may creep into a relationship between you and a team member. To assure that you avoid this difficulty, I recommend the following, decidedly puritanical, "no" rules:

- no flirting of any sort with team members
- no sexual innuendo, comments, or jokes of any kind
- no casual touching
- no disciplining a team member without a witness present
- no sexual relations of any sort with any team member

People cannot choose with whom they fall in love. Should you be foolish enough to ignore the last rule listed above, and you begin a sexual relationship with a person on your team, tell your boss about the relationship *immediately* as this will avoid any accusations that you are secretly favoring your lover at work.

This section on sexual relationships is meant to alert readers in countries where there is a serious risk of complaints of sexual harassment. Readers need to interpret my advice in the light of their own country's legislative and moral climates. What may be acceptable in Italy or Sweden, for example, probably is different from what is acceptable in the United Kingdom, which may well be different from what is acceptable in the United States or India. It is my observation that the situation in all countries seems to be moving in a direction where managers need to be *very careful.*

If you think certain thoughts, are you a racist or a sexual harasser?

Keeping control of what thoughts pass through your head is problematic for many new front-line managers. Perhaps you have wondered along the following lines, "If I find a particular racial characteristic distasteful or annoying, does this make me a racist?" or "If I find someone physically attractive, does that make me a potential sexual harasser?" Regardless of how inappropriate your private thoughts may be, I believe that you should be judged solely on what you do and what you say. What happens in your head is your business alone, but you can rightly be called to account for your actions and your words.

SUMMARY

One difference between average managers and great managers lies in their willingness to face the hard problems of under-performance, misconduct, harassment, and the like.

Two points from the chapter especially warrant review. First, when confronting under-performance, you must find out why the person is not meeting your expectations, and then determine how you can help him or her improve performance. You should, however, know how much time you will give someone to improve. Be patient and supportive until the time limit you have set is reached, but act decisively when the time is up.

Second, when confronting misconduct, you must determine whether there is some underlying problem—a mitigating circumstance—that either partly or fully explains or justifies the behavior. In such a case, the underlying problem itself should be addressed, with the misconduct issue handled in the context of the problem. If you are faced with a straightforward case of misconduct, then you, as front-line manager, must unambiguously and without delay tell the person what he or she is charged with and describe the behavior you expect henceforth. If the person's behavior does not change within whatever time frame you, in consultation with the Personnel or HR department, deem reasonable, or if the misconduct is criminal in nature, you must initiate the appropriate disciplinary proceedings.

When handling difficult problems, you must attain a proper balance between a number of very different, behavioral approaches:

- You must be patient and understanding, but ultimately, after an appropriate length of time, you must act decisively.
- You must not undermine people's self-respect, but you must make them face their problems.
- You must be fair, but you also must apportion your time to staff members in a way that is appropriate to their value to your team.

CHAPTER 3

Managing People in Teams: Leadership Principles

What is leadership? Why is it so frightening? I have given both questions considerable thought over the years since I took my first job as a manager. I think I have answers, but before I attempt even a preliminary definition of leadership, let me list some of the reasons why I believe many new managers find the idea of leadership so scary:

- They worry that they cannot live up to the image of leadership that has been created by the popular culture.
- They fear having responsibility for the long-term survival of the team.
- They panic at having to lead people who are older and more experienced than themselves.
- They shrink at the idea of exercising authority and do not wish to be seen by the team as an authority figure.

By discussing the characteristics essential to leadership, I hope to take some of the fear out of the subject. My intent is to debunk damaging myths about what it takes to be a good leader, and to describe the qualities good leaders should possess.

What Is Leadership?

Leadership, at its simplest, occurs when a person sets the direction and goals for a group of people and leads members of the group toward those goals. When the leader is a front-line manager, the group being led is that manager's team. In order to set goals and propel people toward them, a leader needs to create a *vision* of the future, and to have the *respect* and *trust* of the team so that its members will willingly follow him or her to achieve that vision.

Vision is a creative thing, but the essential bedrock on which your vision must be built is an understanding of the basics of your business. As leader, you must have answers to such questions as: Who are the team's customers? What does your team do that is valued by those customers? How do your customers and your organization measure the performance of your team?

Respect comes to a person who gets things done. Actions speak louder than words, and achievement speaks louder than actions. People respect competence and professionalism in a leader.

Trust comes to a person who is honest and open, whose actions match his or her words, and whose willingness to face difficult issues never flags.

A leader must be endowed with vision, respect, and trust—all lofty attributes—but a leader must also be ready to perform the many different roles associated with front-line management. For example, the leader is the person who makes the tough decisions. The leader creates a community, or culture, within the team. The leader creates the organization within that community and decides who has authority within the team. The leader assures the welfare of the staff. The leader provides the interface between the team and the rest of the organization. The leader is the figurehead of the team.

Although I address various aspects of these many different leadership roles throughout this book, this chapter concentrates on the qualities that underpin good leadership. It also points out a range of common misconceptions about leadership.

LEADERSHIP MYTHS EXPOSED

The first common misconception about leadership is that leaders must "look the part." The notion that leaders should be in the mold of the comic book hero with the square jaw, steady gaze, and firm handshake, is complete nonsense. The Golden Rule of Management tells us that leadership is about what you do and is not about appearances.

The notion that leaders should be in the mold of the comic book hero is complete nonsense.

It is often assumed that leaders must have charisma. Leaders with charismatic personalities certainly have many advantages over people with less flamboyant characters, but if you are such a person, you should be aware of a range of faults that charismatic leaders are prone to have:

- Charismatic leaders tend to create personality cults. Teams can become over-dependent on the leader, the result of which is often harmful if the leader were to leave.
- Charismatic leaders are often poor at delegating.
- Charismatic leaders are often poor listeners; they frequently spend all their time talking.
- Charismatic leaders often have poor self-awareness and hence are not aware of their limitations.
- Charismatic leaders often depend on their personalities to get them out of trouble, so they are not careful enough to avoid getting into trouble.
- Charismatic leaders are often workaholics and may eventually get tired and make too many mistakes.

Charismatic leaders tend to create personality cults.

Another common myth is that leaders need to rely on the authority given to them by the organization. Sure, as the boss, you can order people to do things; but if you are a good leader, you should seldom have to issue a direct order. If you are doing your job properly, your team should want to follow you.

A common failing of authoritarian leaders is that they tend to behave in ways that ensure that nothing is allowed to undermine their authority. Typical examples of how authoritarian leaders behave follow:

- They don't seek advice from the team.
- They don't change their mind or reverse a decision even when it becomes clear that they are wrong.
- They delegate very little in order to avoid diluting their power, and they undermine anyone with delegated authority.
- They intentionally recruit inferior staff members who will never become a threat.
- They use fear, uncertainty, and divide-and-conquer strategies as management techniques to discourage threats to their authority.

There are dozens more characteristics that I could add to the above, but I will stop at five and leave completion of the list as an exercise for the reader. The brief list exaggerates characteristics common to authoritarian leaders, but I think it is worth including because so many of us have a small part of our personality that worries about someone challenging our authority. Although it is unlikely that any authoritarian leaders would ever want to read this book, the discussion helps the rest of us see our borderline behavior for what it is. Whenever we hear a quiet, insidious voice encouraging us to not recruit the outstanding candidate or to not reverse a poor decision, we may recall the message and, hopefully, behave better for it.

The second point in the bulleted list above, concerning reversing bad decisions, states a *management paradox*. A phrase culled from that obscure English dialect called *management-speak*, "paradox" describes the not-uncommon situation in which two factors are in direct conflict. In such a situation, it is desirable to change a bad decision, but it is also desirable not to keep changing decisions because consistency and stability of direction are essential for maintaining staff morale. The resolution of this particular paradox involves ensuring that the basic tenets of the business strategy remain reasonably constant while allowing tactics to change much more frequently.

QUALITIES OF A GOOD LEADER

I begin this section with a warning: Do not allow yourself to become disheartened by what will seem to be a never-ending list of qualities that a great leader should have. You may well think, "There is *nobody* in the whole world who can have all these qualities," and you would be right. However, by emphasizing the many qualities of a good leader—such as vision, communication skills, passion, honesty, integrity, determination, judgment, courageousness, decisiveness, and the like—I intend to provide inspiration for what level you might aspire to, rather than dictate a list of what must be matched. In the next chapter, to help allay the fear many new front-line managers have that they are hopelessly deficient, I discuss techniques that leaders can use to not only manage their weaknesses, but to turn those weaknesses into strengths.

Vision

Vision heads the list. I put it first because I think it is the single most important quality a leader can have. By "vision," I mean determining the strategy for how the team's role and its offerings will evolve over time—matters that are key to the long-term success of the team. Because my focus in this book is on people-related topics, I must warn would-be leaders that a great people-manager with a poor vision is much more dangerous than a manager with a great vision but lousy skills at managing people on the team. Put bluntly, a poor vision, or no vision at all, can be life-threatening to a team.

Far too frequently, managers mistakenly believe that vision is something that only happens at higher levels in the organization. Many front-line managers think of themselves as technicians or scientists rather than as business people, but because every team should deliver some value to its customers—whether those customers are internal to the organization or external—every level of management must have a vision. Shaping a vision can be challenging for many managers, but generalists—that is, people who manage a business area in which they have no professional skills or experience—should be aware that their lack of specific expertise can severely limit them. Clearly, a person who must develop a vision for a business that he or she does not understand from first-hand experience faces a sizable challenge.

What should you do if you find yourself incapable of creating a simple, compelling vision by yourself? Although I would hope such a situation arises only infrequently, if and when it does occur, you will need to engage the appropriate people within your team, and, as a group, brainstorm to create the vision. Indeed, you may want to work with a brainstorming group regardless of whether you have strong views as to what the vision should be.

Leadership does not mean that a manager must generate the fully fleshed-out vision single-handedly, but it does mean he or she should retain the reins. A front-line manager using a group vision-building process should take the lead in defining what properties a good vision (or strategy) has.

So, what is a "good" vision? First, the vision must make sound *business sense:*

- It should be *product-oriented,* clearly depicting the team's current and planned offerings, and listing how they differ from competitors' offerings.
- It should be *market-oriented,* providing a clear view of current and prospective customers.
- It should be *team-based,* building on the team's strengths and capabilities.
- It should be *believable,* identifying achievable goals and the path to realizing them. (Note that a target or goal, such as 25 percent growth per annum, is *not* a vision. A vision must include some description of the strategy

that will allow the team to believe that it is achievable—in this case, that 25 percent growth can be met.)
- It should be *measurable,* showing progress toward accomplishing the vision.

These examples provide only a partial list of ways in which a vision must make business sense because, as I indicated previously, I do not mean to cover business issues in detail in this book.

In addition to making business sense, a vision should be *compelling*—capable of seizing the team's imagination. To do this, it must be clear, simple, and understandable. It must also be both realistic and challenging.

One of the most common reasons managers lack a vision is that developing and pursuing it gets squeezed out by all the urgent issues that bombard them. Vision is important (in fact, it is often the single most important aspect of a leader's job), but it is seldom urgent. As the leader, you will probably need to make a conscious effort to give your vision the "thinking time" it needs.

Your vision can do two very important things. It can underpin the future of the team by defining a potentially successful direction for the team's activities. It can also underpin the morale of the team by giving people a feeling of purpose and a clear sense of direction, *but it will only achieve this second objective if you communicate the vision to your team.*

Communication Skills

It should be obvious that I believe that all managers must be good communicators, but I must now share two slightly depressing observations. First, no matter how well you manage communication within your team, it is likely that most of your team members will feel they are not kept properly informed. Second, under the pressures most managers face, the first thing to suffer usually is communication.

Here are some guidelines to help new managers communicate their vision:

Sell key issues, such as the vision, to your team. You need to sell key issues to your team, using a level of care and planning similar to that which you would use to sell something to a customer. You need to plan the correct mix of written material and presentations. You also need to decide how you are going to establish and maintain a dialogue with your team.

Keep formal communication meetings short, regular, and separate from other routine meetings. Formal communication meetings are truly awful for all concerned—both you and your team will probably despise them. However, such meetings have some invaluable features. First, you put them on your calendar, so they will tend to happen regularly. Second, they show that you are regularly available for complaints to be made directly to you, and as a result, they can release pressures that are building up in the team. A common mistake many new front-line managers make is to allow the agony to drag on—I suggest you adhere to a rigid time limit of one hour or less.

One of the most difficult issues you will face is how to pass on to your team the information you receive from higher levels in the organization. Although I address this issue in detail later in the book, I mention it here because it is a focal point of many formal communication meetings.

Ensure that matters that directly affect staff members are discussed with them before irrevocable decisions are made. It is a fact that people who feel that they have no control over their environment become anxious, stressed, and de-motivated. Consequently, staff members who find out that decisions that affect them directly have been made without their knowledge or input tend to react badly. I suggest you make such matters your top communication priority. Remember that you do not have to convey all information personally; you can use other members of your team's organization as appropriate. However, it is good practice to make sure that you give bad news personally.

Use e-mail to communicate with your team. E-mail is a really efficient mechanism for short, chatty updates, and is also a good way to solicit people's views. Many people are comfortable sending the boss an e-mail when they might not be comfortable mentioning the matter in person or in a memo.

A word of warning, however: Triple-check *your* e-mail messages carefully to ensure that team members cannot misinterpret them. More than once, I have seen managers unintentionally offend team members with carelessly worded e-mail messages. I would also advise against giving bad news via e-mail, because it may well be interpreted as the coward's option.

Communicate using a two-way process. When you make yourself available so that people on your team can ask you questions, make sure to ask them questions as well. Regularly scheduling one-on-one meetings with staff members will provide a moderately formal setting for people to ask you questions and also will afford you the opportunity to probe their views. If you are one of those lucky people who are naturally good listeners, two-way communication will be easy; if you are like the rest of us, keep practicing those listening skills. Another helpful strategy is to organize your team to include someone to oversee, or assist you with, staff development. That person can provide feedback on problems within the team, and can alert you to serious concerns before they blow up into major issues.

Make yourself available for informal questions as well as formal. If members of your team see that you are not hiding away from their questions, they are much less likely to think you might keep things from them. You must expect that at least some members even of normal, healthy teams will probably foster fairly high levels of paranoia and theories of conspiracy, and you must constantly work to damp down such negative feelings.

Communicate decisions quickly. When you have made an important decision, you need to communicate that decision quickly, before rumors start. Einstein's Theory of Relativity tells us that nothing can travel faster than light, but apparently the theory doesn't apply to rumors. Work out whom to brief, in what order, and then do it immediately.

Passion

Welcome to the most rewritten section in this book. Why has the subject of passion caused me so many problems? Being brutally honest as I look back over my career in management (which so far has lasted more than ten years), I have to admit that the worst mistakes I have made were committed in the name of "passion," by which I mean enthusiasm both for the job to be done and for the long-term vision. However, if there is a personality trait that distinguishes a true leader from someone who is just a manager, I believe it is passion. It is often a leader's passion and enthusiasm that inspire the team to follow him or her toward the vision. Passion is also the quality that causes a leader to drive through the obstacles and setbacks that would stop someone less passionate. The problems leaders run into arise when too much passion results in irrational, intolerant, or aggressive behavior.

The irrational side of passion: I can best explain the irrational side of passion by giving an example. Imagine the not-unlikely situation in which a leader's vision encompasses the development of a new product or offering. If the leader becomes extremely passionate about that offering, it is all too easy for him or her to be unrealistic about its chances of success and failure. Failure is likely when the leader becomes unable to see that, from a customer's perspective, the offering has severe limitations.

The intolerant side of passion: Leaders who are passionate tend to polarize their view of people into two camps—those who support them, and those who are against them. Put another way, they see two sorts of people: "them" and "us." Such a view tends to make outsiders regard the leader and the team as arrogant and insular.

The aggressive side of passion: Passionate people often see people who get in their way as opponents to be defeated. I am embarrassed to admit that more than once I have interpreted perfectly normal, organizational bureaucracy as a plot to destroy my team. More embarrassing is the fact that at times I have even fought against my organization's goals. Such ill-advised battles are seldom won; instead, they create a bad reputation for the leader and the team as troublemakers.

Honesty

It is hard for a leader to retain the respect of team members if they discover that they cannot rely on their leader to tell them the truth. The difficulty in always being completely truthful is that honesty is not a black-and-white issue. Elsewhere in the book, I discuss times when you, as a leader, should reveal less than the whole truth, and even times (such as when you are required to toe the corporate line) when you might actually have to stretch the truth in the direction of a bare untruth. However, my advice is: *Be as honest as you possibly can.*

No matter what happens, do not get sucked into telling "little lies." It can be very tempting to be economical with the truth, or to bend the truth just a little, when asked by someone on the team, or by your boss, to explain your actions. Little lies are so tempting because they allow you to paint the situation in a somewhat more favorable light, or to avoid raising an issue that you would rather not discuss in detail. Don't do it! Little lies are the thin end of the wedge and can easily trip you up, seriously damaging your credibility.

To say that a leader or team member possesses the quality of honesty implies that the person refuses to lie to, steal from, or deceive anyone at any time, but it also suggests a nearly synonymous quality that is another necessary attribute of a good leader: integrity.

Integrity

Integrity is an attribute to be treasured and cultivated in a leader. In my opinion, the four top qualities of a good leader are vision, determination, judgment, and integrity. I regard them as essential qualities because a leader's vision and determination are key to keeping the team in business, and his or her judgment and integrity earn the respect of the team.

People assume that integrity is a quality that either you have or you don't. However, I don't believe this to be the case. I believe that it is difficult, but still possible, to develop a complex behavior such as integrity. It is a fact that much of our behavior is learned rather than innate. Although most of our learning occurs when we are young, there is no reason why as adults we cannot learn new behavior. Try a simple exercise: If you are naturally parsimonious, it is fairly easy to train yourself to put your hand in your pocket and pull out enough money to buy your fair share—or more than your fair share—of drinks at social gatherings.

But what about integrity? Can you train yourself to always do the right thing. As I attempt to address that question, I am reminded of a joke about acting: "The most important thing about good acting is sincerity—once you have learned to fake that, you have cracked it." Can you fake integrity? My view is that most leaders know what their staff members will consider to be right and what they will consider to be wrong. If I am correct, then a leader can consciously do what the team will consider to be the right thing.

The matter of developing integrity beyond that with which you, as a leader, are naturally endowed raises two important questions: First, won't your staff spot that you are faking it if your integrity level is learned, not innate? Second, is it possible to change such a fundamental characteristic of your personality as integrity?

Of course the answer to the first question is yes. Your team members will spot that you are acting—but they are likely to admire you for it. They will see acting as an effort on your part to behave well. Perhaps more scary than the idea that they will see that you are acting is the suspicion that you probably will start off being an embarrassingly bad actor. With practice, however, you can become a good actor. With enough time, you may find that you have achieved your goal and that you are no longer acting!

The answer to the second question is also yes. This acting technique works most easily on simple aspects of your behavior. It is much more challenging to fake complex aspects of your personality. For example, a hyperintense, competitive personality is likely to find it impossible to stop wanting to compete, but it should be possible for such a person to be less aggressively competitive.

Determination

In the final analysis, a leader should be judged by what he or she has achieved—hopefully as the driver behind a multitude of successful team efforts. Determination, the drive to achieve a vision, plays a major role in what can be achieved.

Is there anything you as a front-line manager can do to improve your level of determination? The best technique I have found to increase my own level of determination is to designate others in my team to nag me to make things happen.

Judgment

The average day in the life of the average manager is punctuated by the need to make numerous, mostly small, decisions. To rise above the level of the average manager, a leader must make lots and lots of *good* decisions—a process facilitated by good judgment. The ability to judge fairly and quickly generally improves with experience, but it is my contention that good judgment also must come naturally. That is to say, judgment is a quality that either you've got or you haven't. Putting it bluntly, a leader who makes too many wrong decisions will lose the respect of the team, and should be moved to a job for which he or she is better suited.

If you are fortunate enough to have been born with good judgment, or if you have cultivated it through the trials and tribulations of on-the-job experience, you still need to remember that you have to be around to exercise it. I have observed that a leader who is out of the office too often will lose the team's respect because he or she is not there to make decisions when decisions need to be made. Good leaders will have to say no to many demands on their time.

Courage and Decisiveness

As well as needing to make the right decisions, a front-line manager must be willing to make the difficult decisions. The Golden Rule of Management says that you will be judged by your actions. There is, however, a corollary of the Golden Rule:

You will be judged by your inactions as much as by your actions.

The corollary refers not only to those occasions when a manager chooses not to make a decision, but also to situations in which making the decision is avoided because the manager will not even acknowledge the underlying problem that the decision would address. For example, a front-line manager who postpones confronting an under-performing staff member surely will be judged unfavorably.

*You will be judged by your inactions
as much as by your actions.*

The line that divides a leader who is decisive from one who shoots from the hip is narrow indeed. One reason experienced leaders usually outperform less experienced managers is that they know when to take the time to think a problem through, and when they have to make a snap decision.

How willing should you be to change your decisions? Some managers seem to believe that changing a decision is a sign of weakness, whereas I believe that reversing a bad decision is more often a sign of strength. What should you do, however, if you find that even as you gain experience, you need to keep changing your decisions? I am sorry to be brutal, but frequent reversals are a clear sign that a manager has poor judgment and should be looking for a different type of job.

Responsibility

The team gets all the credit. The manager gets all the blame. It may not seem fair, but those are the rules of the game. I noted previously that you must not allow your superiors to go directly to your staff to criticize or chastise anyone, but the point bears repeating here. You may ask your superiors to deal directly with individual team members when praising them for a success; you must insist, however, that your superiors deal only with you regarding any problems with your team. Assure your managers that you will sort matters out, and that you take responsibility for any problems. In addition, be certain to let your managers know that if there is any punishment to be handed out, you must do it personally. Your people have a right to expect you to represent their best interests in dealings with the rest of the organization, and by claiming blame but not credit, you show that you truly support them.

Consistent and Open–Minded Responses

When putting together this list of qualities that a good leader should have, I initially included reasonableness. On reflection, however, I concluded that although people generally expect their leaders to be consistent and open-minded in their treatment of staff and issues, they do not expect them to be reasonable at all times. In fact, if you think about the behavior of great leaders throughout history, I suspect you will join me in concluding that many of them were far from reasonable—indeed, quite a few of them may have been stark, raving mad.

Composure

Leaders who panic when faced with an emergency or who overreact to minor problems quickly lose the respect of even the least experienced team member. Equally problematic are leaders who leave decision-making to the last minute and hence create crises due to poor planning. Good leaders should promote thoughtful responses to problems, and should never spread panic throughout the team.

Delegation Skills

Good leaders know that no matter how well organized they are and no matter how hard they work, there are not enough hours in the day to do everything that needs to be done. The principal way of solving this problem is to delegate roles and tasks to other people. Unfortunately, delegation is easier said than done.

What factors make effective delegation so difficult? One factor is *knowledge of context*. Recall that, in my introductory chapter, I included a Literal-Reading Warning to caution the reader to interpret my advice according to *the unique context within which he or she works*. In order to delegate effectively, the manager must understand the context within which responsibility is passed to a team member.

A second element essential to successful delegation is *clarity*. Defining exactly what responsibilities and authority you have delegated can be difficult, but if delegation is to work, then you must invest significant thought and time in being unambiguous. It is inevitable that you will have to refine role and task definitions as you go along, but this job will be made easier if clear communications exist between delegator and delegatee.

Third among the elements is the *trustworthiness* of the delegatee. You must assess to what degree you can trust the person to perform the job you have delegated. All too often, you may find yourself in a position in which you must delegate responsibility, but you either do not know whether you can depend upon the person (perhaps because he or she has little or no track record in performing the task) or you have reasons to distrust the person.

If you do not know whether you can fully trust the person to perform the task competently, then you will need to take precautionary measures: First, you must determine what level of visibility and control will allow you to monitor progress; in conjunction with this, you also need to decide whether you can afford to have the person fail and what you will need to do if he or she does fail. Second, you must consider what level of support an inexperienced person, tackling a new responsibility for the first time, will need. If appropriate, you may wish to assign a coach or mentor to assist the person.

If you have reason to doubt that the person can perform the delegated role but delegation seems unavoidable, you will need to take the same measures as in the preceding scenario: You will want to install additional visibility and control measures, and formulate a contingency plan to be activated in the event the person does fail. By thinking through every detail, you should be able to decide at what point it would be more cost-effective not to delegate. As you evaluate the pros and cons, determine whether there is anything the person can do to increase your confidence—and then ask yourself why you have not provided leadership in that direction.

Many managers labor under the common misconception that delegation is a black-and-white issue, and think that there is no point in delegating tasks to someone if you are going to have to monitor that person constantly. It is my view that the fourth element essential to successful delegation is maintaining *the right level of visibility and control.* In your role as front-line manager, you should maintain a level of supervision appropriate to the person's experience and track record. It is worth discussing related topics with the person to whom you delegate, such as what level of control you will be exercising. This is far better than the not-uncommon situation in which a manager sends someone off to perform a task unsupervised and then panics when something goes wrong, responding either by taking responsibility off the person or by putting draconian controls in place.

Part of maintaining the right level of visibility and control involves assessing what kind of damage a person might do if he or she fails in properly performing the task you have delegated. I recommend that even before you delegate, you ask yourself what damage could incur with failure. If the answer is that failure will inflict major damage, then you must raise this issue with the person before he or she begins the delegated task. Openly discuss what action you will take if the person encounters major problems. If you go ahead with your plan to delegate to this person, supervise closely so that the person knows the level of support you will provide.

The fifth element that can make delegation difficult is the fact that *different people perform the same job differently.* You may have to school yourself not to interfere if someone does a task very differently from the way you would have done it. If you see problems with the way someone is doing a job, then you may wish to alert the individual to the dangers as you see them, but if the individual has proven to be both responsible and fully competent to perform the task, then he or she must be allowed to make the final choice of how to do the job.

For delegation to be effective, you must *take every precaution not to undermine the person to whom you have assigned authority.* This sixth factor is one of the most difficult to control because, as a front-line manager, you may inadvertently undermine people to whom you have delegated authority. Some examples of ways in which a manager unintentionally may undermine a worker's ability to do the job follow:

- failing to give the subordinate all the information that he or she will need to do the job properly—the context in which the work will be performed, for example
- failing to stop people who have more experience or more seniority from interfering
- neglecting to state unambiguously and often that the person can come to you for advice and support
- conspicuously attending meetings at which the person should be taking the lead (if you—the individual's manager—are there, people at the meeting will naturally look to you for decisions)
- criticizing the person in public
- making decisions that either the individual should make or about which he or she should be consulted
- putting in excessive or inadequate visibility and controls
- taking an interest in unnecessary details
- belittling the way in which the individual performs a task or role
- meddling—for example, by discussing the delegated work with other team members
- changing the ground rules

There are, of course, additional factors that make delegation difficult, but the preceding paragraphs describe the problems I have encountered most frequently in my years as a manager of both IT staff and research scientists. Awareness of these factors, considered in combination with two simple guidelines, should help you delegate more successfully.

Delegation Guideline #1: Define success and failure criteria at the time you delegate. People need to know if they are doing the task or role in a way that is satisfactory. It is essential that you provide well-defined success and failure criteria at the time you delegate a job, but also give periodic, informal feedback on how the person is doing as time goes on.

Delegation Guideline #2: Avoid delegating in response to a crisis. I often see managers delegating tasks only when they become overloaded. I hope I have made it clear that delegating a task needs a considerable amount of care and preparation— exactly the sort of thing you will not do if you are under pressure. It is much better to delegate tasks prior to becoming overloaded than to delegate out of desperation. If you have no other option but to delegate in response to an urgent situation, then you need to take sufficient time to do it properly; if you choose to rush it, don't come to me for sympathy when it all goes wrong!

SUMMARY

Leadership is not about appearances. It does not matter whether you can talk the talk; what matters is that you can walk the walk.

A good leader knows where the team must be directed (the vision) and has the respect and trust of staff members. As a result of the leader's clear articulation of the vision, the team will willingly follow.

In this chapter, I have presented a daunting but achievable list of qualities that I believe a good leader should have. I stated that I consider the top four leadership qualities to be vision, determination, judgment, and integrity, followed by attributes such as courage, decisiveness, good communication skills, honesty, the ability to delegate, the ability to accept responsibility, consistency, open-mindedness, and composure.

I also described one particular quality that has very strong positive aspects, but brings with it great risks: passion. Passion can be the greatest of all motivators for a team, but it can also make people behave in irrational, intolerant, and aggressive ways. As a front-line manager, be wary of misdirected passion.

CHAPTER 4

Managing the Practice of Team Leadership

When I finished writing the preceding chapter, I realized that I was feeling depressed—I was uncertain about whether I possess a requisite number of leadership qualities. To help put things in perspective, I compared the qualities a great leader should possess with my own. You have probably guessed that the lists were different. I realized what I needed to do was analyze how *real people* lead in the *real world*. This chapter treats the practice of leadership.

LEADERSHIP STYLE

I previously identified vision, determination, integrity, and judgment as the cornerstones of leadership. These four qualities are extremely valuable, but I do not want to leave you with the impression that a good leader must have *all* these qualities. One of the reasons that managers survive despite their flaws and inadequacies is that they adopt a style that accentuates their positive qualities to such an extent that their team will forgive their shortcomings.

If you think about famous, contemporary, corporate executives, you will realize that a number have survived on vision and total determination alone; others have succeeded by means of determination and a fanatical attention to detail; while still others have tied their success to integrity, charm, and a great ability to delegate. From such examples of corporate success, we can see that there is no single, correct leadership style; great leaders are made from a combination of many distinctive components. The lesson to be learned here is, whatever combination of leadership qualities you may possess or cultivate, applying the following techniques can help you become a stronger leader:

- Identify your *strengths* and build your leadership style around them.
- Identify your *weaknesses* and assemble a support team to compensate for your weaknesses and to whose members you can delegate roles that you are ill-equipped to perform.
- Take a management job that plays to your strengths and that builds on qualities that border on being weaknesses. For example, a person who has great analytical skills but verges on being cold and sometimes dictatorial can be ideal for turning a failing team around.

The Young Leader

Most first-time managers face the daunting prospect of having authority over staff members who are older and more experienced than themselves. As a newly promoted manager, keep in mind that you are probably more worried about supervising people senior to you than they are. It is unlikely that you are the first young manager they have had to train, and most experienced staff will try not to embarrass or undermine you, provided you follow a few simple rules.

Organize the team to make best use of the experience available to you. Experienced staff members will expect to be consulted. If you do not seek their views, they will think that you are either arrogant or insecure. Ultimately, you must make the decisions yourself, but you should make well-informed decisions.

Avoid making snap decisions too soon after taking over.
When taking over a team, try to give yourself time to find out about the team, its business, and some of its history before trying to change things.

Be very careful when criticizing experienced staff. If you need to discuss a shortcoming in an experienced team member's performance, make it clear that you have tried to be very careful to get your facts right. Criticizing a person when you don't have the facts straight is not only potentially embarrassing, it also can jeopardize your standing with the team. If you are careful to treat experienced staff members with respect and show that you are trying to find out what went wrong so that they and you can learn from the experience, they will probably help you by criticizing themselves first.

Be very careful when criticizing experienced staff.

LEADERSHIP ROLES

Some of the roles for which a leader must take responsibility should already be clear from the preceding discussion of leadership qualities (for example, the role of creating the vision and business strategy for the team). In this section, I describe other key roles, starting with two roles that, if performed badly, can contribute to your becoming an *ex*-leader.

Good bottom-line management

No matter how superior your vision, people skills, and ability to communicate, sooner or later you will be expected to agree to a budget and then deliver your program within that budget. If you believe you will not be able to keep within the budget but must accept it anyway, document your objections and provide a detailed alternative. The last thing you should do is expect your management to be tolerant if you exceed your budget. Your team may find the whole business of meeting the budget a bore, and some team members may even moan about your meanness (financial probity is nearly always interpreted as meanness), but your job and theirs could well depend on delivering within budget. Insist that everyone you manage make the effort to work with you in managing the financial bottom line. To help you with this difficult role, I provide some practical advice later in this book—in Chapter 9, "Organizing Your Team (and Yourself)."

Legal and regulatory compliance

Ensure that all legal and regulatory issues are handled properly. Health regulations, safety and code violations, and such legal issues as discrimination, negligence, and the like, can threaten your career and your team's future. You ignore them at your peril!

Key-task supervision

If problems take you by surprise, it most probably is *your* fault. You need to monitor key tasks so that you can spot problems in time to take corrective action. You also need to ask searching questions to expose less visible problems, such as a collapse in morale that may lead to mass resignations.

External-threat assessment

Many threats to a team's existence come from changes in the environment in which the team operates, and one of the roles a front-line manager must perform is to scan the external environment for such threats. Changes in the external environment might occur as a result of a discontinuous change in the market to which the team sells its products and services—a period of rapid growth coming to an end, a new type of product displacing your team's product, or a new piece of government regulation, for example—or it could be a reorganization that will reduce your team's influence in your organization. It is the leader's responsibility to ensure that all threatening changes in the external environment are identified and addressed.

Team–customer interface management

Because the team-customer interface delivers value from your team to the customer, it is one of the most important assets your team has. The Golden Rule of Management means that unless you are active in ensuring that the interaction between the team and your customers has your highest priority, then it will not be a high priority of the team.

Pace control

Some teams develop an energy level and a pace that ensure that things get done fast, and problems get sorted out quickly. This property, which I refer to as momentum, usually reflects the leader's decision-making style. If you sort problems quickly, and chase issues that seem to have stalled, then you can raise the pace of the team.

Priority setting

One of the realities of management is that you can only accomplish a few major tasks at any one time. In addition, there usually are only a few areas in which a team can be truly outstanding. Taking on the task of focusing the team and setting priorities is difficult for many front-line managers. Don't let yourself be intimidated—rather, start things off by making sure that the team has only one or two priorities. Then, help team members to focus on them. As you become more experienced, you will need to diligently maintain a balance between short-term pressures and longer-term objectives, being careful to guard against the danger that urgent tasks will push accomplishment of more important, longer-term objectives too far into the future.

Quality assurance

A leader should make it clear that the value the team delivers to its customers is paramount. To assure the highest value, the leader must be directly involved in assuring the quality of the team's outputs. It is very easy for a team to become introspective and to focus on process—how things are done—rather than on product—what is being produced. One way the leader can help the team focus on real value is to personally review, evaluate, and, to whatever degree is necessary, control the quality of the team's outputs.

In my own line of business as a consultant and as a manager of research scientists, I preview nearly all reports that are to be delivered to my client's or team's customers. I do this because I believe my review of the material will help assure the relevance and accuracy of those reports. Personal involvement is almost universally effective because most fields require a level of accuracy and relevance similar to that required in my business. Most front-line managers can monitor quality by getting involved in some of the operations of their team.

Operations that involve direct interaction with the customer are particularly suited to personal intervention, a point made vivid to me in the town where I live. There, at a supermarket recognized for its excellent service and high-quality foods, I have occasionally seen the store manager packing customers' groceries, restocking shelves, and serving in the bakery, all the while chatting informally with customers. I do not think

85

that the outstanding service provided by that supermarket is an accident.

A more general way to interpret the meaning of the preceding is, *a manager's actions set the expectations of the team.* This is a result of the Golden Rule of Management: If you personally work very hard, then the team will work very hard. If you are scrupulously honest, then the team will tend to be very honest. Every aspect of your own behavior sets the level of expectation you have for the team.

Pattern- and trend-spotting

As front-line manager, you will probably have a better overview of your team's activities than any other individual in the organization. Because of this unique vantage point, you may be able to spot patterns in problems that impede productivity, such as a particular mistake that keeps being made. You may also be in a position to predict trends in their earliest stage of development, seeing, for example, when customers are beginning to want a change in your team's product or service.

OPPORTUNITIES FOR LEADERSHIP

There are times when being the leader demands that you take a prominent role. If you fail to take the lead, your position at the head of the pack may be seriously jeopardized. In the following two sections, I describe some of the times when a leader should demonstrate his or her ability to lead.

Work crises

Many different types of crisis can require a manager to step up and take charge, but some of the most disruptive include *last-minute, rush deadlines* and *serious complaints received from disgruntled customers.* At such times, you, as front-line manager, may need to take control of how your team responds to the crisis. Some of the key issues you will need to address include the following:

86

- You need to prevent panic from breaking out.
- You need to ensure that a thoughtful response is made. To do this, you must find out what the real issues are, so that you respond to the real problem rather than to symptoms of the problem.
- You need to perform a "worst case" analysis and ensure that your response is consistent with the damage that the team may suffer. This analysis will help you determine how hard, fast, and extreme your response must be. You may need contingency plans in case the worst case actually happens; in addition, you must decide whether the crisis is serious enough that you need to brief your boss.
- You need to avoid making impossible promises, such as committing to sorting out a problem within too short a period of time. Give yourself some leeway and then sort the problem out faster than you predicted.
- You need to decide how open to be with the people affected by the problem. Remember that the less you tell people, the more they are likely to imagine problems that do not exist.
- You need to be willing to share in the team's pain, either by immediately rolling up your sleeves and helping or, if that is not practical, by working late on your own tasks as team members work late on theirs.
- You need to be supportive, either by being there to offer advice and encouragement or by being compassionate and sending people home if they are exhausted, making sure they eat regularly, and the like.
- You need to be there to accept full responsibility for any problems and to protect your team members from being personally criticized.

Crises, although surely not to be invited, provide great opportunities for impressing people. Most customers accept that everyone messes up once in a while, and the way a manager responds to a crisis can enhance the trust that people have in the manager *and in the team*. The old cliché stating "when the going gets tough, the tough get going" is very true.

Change management

The rate at which companies need to adapt to rapidly changing business requirements accelerated dramatically throughout the 1990s and shows no sign of abating as the twenty-first century unfolds. In most organizations today, to stand still is to invite extinction, making the management of change critical to the organization's survival.

Within the front-line manager's jurisdiction, change management consists primarily of handling change *as it affects the team*. As manager, you must recognize that change imposed from on high will create feelings of pressure and stress within team members. It is perfectly normal for the initial responses to change to be anger and rejection. Allow your staff sufficient time to move through these initial, negative emotions, but be prepared to intervene if anyone seems to carry the burden of anger too long. One way you can defuse negative feelings is by showing that you will personally face your share, or more than your share, of the pain and grief that accompany the change.

Although you must never waver from a position that change itself is nonnegotiable, make it clear that you will do everything you reasonably can to manage the implementation of that change so as to reduce unnecessary pain and disruption. You need to consult with those affected, without making it seem as if you are giving them an option as to whether the change will be imposed. There is a delicate balance to be struck between soliciting people's views and giving the mistaken impression that they have the power to dictate to you exactly how the change is to be implemented.

THE BANK-ACCOUNT CONCEPT OF LEADERSHIP

I expect that many readers are beginning to feel a bit daunted by the thought of what they must do to excel as a leader. Can anyone live up to the standard I am describing? Of course the answer is no, for even the greatest leaders have off days. A good way to think about leadership is as a kind of bank account: When you do something right, you bank some credibility with your team in the form of points you can draw on at a later date. The bad news is that your deposits (the good things you do) count less than your withdrawals (your mistakes), so it is easy to go bankrupt; the good news is that you can make some mistakes without totally losing your credibility as the leader.

Withdrawals and deposits

Although this book is almost entirely about the qualities that make a person a good leader and a good manager, this section calls specific attention to some mistakes that, if made, will damage your reputation—true withdrawals from your leadership bank account—and it highlights some easily overlooked techniques for enhancing your image as a leader.

Don't be afraid to roll your sleeves up and help. Many managers themselves used to perform some of their team members' roles before they became managers. If you find yourself in the position of needing to help out, do so. Even if your professional expertise is not in the areas of the team's business, you undoubtedly have some relevant presentational, organizational, or business-related skills to contribute. Working alongside your team, delivering value to your customers, will show you a view of your team you cannot get from just being the boss, and can greatly increase the respect team members will have for you.

Don't think you are too important to do menial jobs. A willingness to do menial jobs, such as making the coffee or washing the teapot, will strengthen, not undermine, your authority. If you do menial tasks, do them as well as possible. At my office, we decided that senior staff members should take responsibility for coffee break, and so I volunteered to be the provisioning officer. It is a small job, but I pride myself on buying supplies as cheaply as possible, and ensuring that we never run out of anything.

Don't be seduced by signs of status. The personal secretary, reserved parking space, plush office, and other manifestations of upper management are not appropriate to your position as a front-line manager. Enjoying such perks will undermine your leadership. If you inherit them, get rid of them, either openly—if your organization will allow it—or quietly, for example by telling team members that the secretary is there to support the entire team, by using your parking space as a visitors' space, or by ensuring that your office is set up to serve as a meeting room whenever you are not in it.

Don't give in to self-serving behavior. If members of your team detect that furthering your career is your top priority, they will never trust you. If you are very ambitious and know it would be dishonest to act otherwise, you need to decide whether your long-term interests are best served by being a good leader or whether they will be better served in some other capacity. If you decide they are compatible, you will need to squelch any urge to adopt crude short-term tactics for promoting yourself. Your team's trust is essential to your success as leader.

Don't deny your mistakes. Many managers worry about losing face when they make mistakes and, as a result, try to cover them up. Don't be like them. Your reputation can only be enhanced by your putting your hands up, admitting the error, and apologizing, as appropriate. If you are making so many mistakes that admitting them is not a viable strategy, then it is time to try a job for which you are better suited.

Don't try to be liked. Do not confuse being respected with being liked. Put bluntly, it is essential that you are respected, and irrelevant if you are liked. Courting popularity is an excellent recipe for damaging your ability to be an effective leader.

Don't try to be "one of the gang." Regrettably, the trite comment about it being lonely at the top has considerable truth behind it. As a leader, you can never fully be one of the team, and at social gatherings the people you supervise will quite correctly never completely forget you are their boss.

Don't be a tightwad. Other than perhaps a comptroller or the chief financial officer of your company, no one likes a tightwad. In a corporate setting, the distaste for miserly behavior is especially pronounced when the tightwad may well be both the best-paid person on the team and the person whose success depends on the hard work of *all* team members. I am thinking here about your personal generosity, or lack thereof. Do you remember the birthdays of support staff? Do you buy staff members Christmas presents? When you go on trips overseas, do you bring back thoughtful gifts? When at social gatherings, are you generous in buying drinks? Do you subsidize social gatherings from bonuses you get?

Don't tolerate bullying behavior. I hope I do not have to convince any front-line manager that overt bullying is a bad trait, but equally reprehensible are the subtle forms of bullying, such as talking in such a way as to overrule people, losing your temper frequently, and commenting on a team member's weaknesses in front of his or her peers. Be careful not to be a bully yourself, and also make it clear that you will not tolerate bullying among members of your staff.

Don't be an absentee manager. There surely are exceptions to the following, but it is my opinion that a leader who is not highly visible to his or her team cannot be a truly good leader. To be the best, you must be available to the team on a daily basis—or as close to daily as you can arrange. In order to avoid spending excessive time away from the team, you probably will need to decline as many invitations to meetings that take you out of the office as you reasonably can. The reality of front-line management is that you must weigh your desire to be off-site (where you may have a real opportunity to learn in the presence of more experienced managers, including even your own supervisors, whose invitations to meetings will be politically difficult to decline) against your need to be on-site, accessible 24-7 to your team. To maximize accessibility when you are in the office, make sure you spend time talking to staff members face-to-face. Make yourself available for ad-hoc questions by regularly having coffee or lunch with the team, for example.

Don't imply that a job you do not do, or cannot do, is easy. If you do not respect your staff members, it is likely that they will not respect you. It's as simple as that! I suspect that some of you are sitting there thinking that of course you respect your staff, but what I am talking about includes respect for such intangibles as an individual's time, special skills, and sense of self-worth. If you have any doubt, just check that you have not said anything like the following:

- "Surely all you need to do is ..."
- "This shouldn't take you long ..."
- "I've got an easy job I would like you to do for me ..."
- "Don't bother me with details ..."
- "It's only a small change ..."
- "I think this will solve your problem ..."
- "I can do that on my PC at home, so it should be pretty easy for you to do here ..."
- "Stop raising difficulties. I want solutions, not problems ..."

Don't settle for the easy compromise. One of your jobs as front-line leader is to make the team's hard decisions. It is also your role to actively seek out problems by asking challenging questions. Often, the seemingly reasonable approach of trying to find the middle ground and making a measured response will just delay the inevitable disaster. You need to know when to get off the fence and take a stand. In my experience, it is more common to make a mistake by underreacting than by overreacting. It has also been my experience that staff members are often very supportive of clear, decisive action in the appropriate circumstances.

Don't micromanage. You must give your staff members space to grow. As is the case with respect, if you do not trust them, they will never trust you. Occasionally diving down into the detail will help show that you care about the detail, and will also help keep people on their toes. However, the converse, constantly diving down into the detail, is one of the most irritating habits a leader can exhibit.

Don't underestimate the importance of the team's perception of you. Be aware that it is very likely that team members do not perceive you as you intend. Possibly those perceptions will be unfair, but when did fair have anything to do with life? Remember the following truth:

Perceptions are the only reality.

In addition, if you have someone to whom you can delegate personnel management, do so; he or she can be an important source of feedback. I also suggest that whenever staff members leave the team, you conduct an exit interview, and use it as an opportunity to discover how you are perceived.

WHEN TO MOVE ON

Different circumstances call for different leadership styles. For example, turning around a failing team requires a very different approach from the approach needed to build or grow a successful team, which requires a different approach from running a team that is neither growing nor contracting, and so on. You need to recognize when a team is moving from one phase to another, because at the very least, you will have to adapt your leadership style. Be prepared for the possibility that you may need to move aside and let a new leader take over.

The very best leaders foster an organization that is not overly dependent on their own personal skills, and will think about succession planning to ensure a smooth transition to new leadership at the appropriate time.

SUMMARY

Given that few human beings can hope to have all, or even most, of the qualities of a truly good leader, how can we cope with our shortcomings? There are a number of techniques you can adopt as you strengthen yourself as a leader:

- Develop a leadership style that accentuates your positive qualities.
- Delegate responsibilities for which you have little talent to others in the team who are better suited to handle them than you.
- Do enough things right that your team will forgive your mistakes—what I call the bank-account concept of leadership.
- Fake it. (By this I mean that if you do not naturally behave in what the team would regard as a principled way, then use your intellect to force yourself to do what your team will think are the right things.)

CHAPTER 5

Project Management

I began writing this book with someone like me in mind. That might seem a bit egocentric, but let me explain. What I mean is that, initially, I focused my attention on *people like me*. For example:

- people who work in largish organizations
- people who manage skilled or professional workers
- people who lead teams of up to thirty workers

There are, of course, other details about the audience I first envisioned, but as I wrote, I kept the people described above clearly in mind. When I completed my draft manuscript, I sent it off to a vast number of friends, relatives, and colleagues, many of whom did not fit my audience profile. From them, I discovered that much of what I discuss seems relevant not just to "people like me," but also to people who work in small companies, to managers of so-called blue-collar workers, and even to people who oversee one or two others but don't consider themselves to be managers.

Learning of this additional audience was very encouraging, especially since I (like most authors, I suspect) secretly hope that the universe—in its entirety—will be my eventual audience. That market-view bubble burst unceremoniously when feedback from some readers who manage project teams, rather than organizational teams, was not as complimentary. Initially, I found this puzzling, but the more I explored the distinction between project management and management of a team whose existence is not tied to a specific project, the more I came to see very substantial differences.

Whole books—possibly numbering in the thousands—have been devoted to the subject of project management, so my discussion in this one brief chapter is intended to do little more than introduce the subject in the context of my particular viewpoint. That's okay; I intend merely to give the principles that underpin good project management in order to identify the major differences between project management and management of a team. If this topic does not interest you, move on to the next chapter—all chapters that follow concentrate on the management and leadership of a team within the management structure of an organization.

If the preceding paragraph contains a hint of disclaimer, now comes the point when I must issue a bona fide warning: I believe myself to be sufficiently competent as a manager to write this book, but I must confess that I am, at best, only an average *project* manager. Writing this chapter has required both research and gumption. Fortunately, I have worked on many very-well-managed projects—and a few less-well-managed ones—and have based this chapter on an analysis of my experiences.

PROJECT MANAGEMENT VERSUS ORGANIZATIONAL MANAGEMENT

There are a number of significant differences between leading a project team and managing people whose work is not tied to a specific project, as the following sections describe.

Projects last for a fixed duration; organizational teams have no set life span. The leader of a team that is part of an organization's structure is in some sense the leader of a tribe, and the leader's prime objective is the long-term survival of the tribe. As a consequence, his or her behavior will be judged in terms of whether it is good for the tribe's survival. In contrast, the project manager's job is to deliver the project's objective, on time and within budget—after which, the job is over. Because project team members know that a successful project will end, they will accept behavior from their project manager that they would find unacceptable in a team leader.

Dictatorial behavior may be acceptable for project managers, but it is unacceptable in team leaders. I have worked on projects where the project manager appeared to have adopted the people-management style of Genghis Khan, but the team accepted this style and worked hard and enthusiastically to deliver the project as directed. I think that one of the reasons for this is that, on projects, people accept that the manager is sometimes correct in acting as if the end justifies the means.

Dictatorial behavior may be acceptable.

Team culture is less important to projects than to teams. A project manager may well want to build team spirit, but establishing a long-lived tribal culture, based on well-defined "beliefs," is not essential. Although anyone attempting to get a job done benefits from the cooperation that a healthy and cohesive culture fosters, many of the issues I discuss later—in the chapter on team cultures—will be less relevant to a project manager. This difference in the importance of culture results from the basic difference between each group's fundamental nature.

Project members have a clearly defined objective; team members accomplish a multitude of related and unrelated tasks. Project managers tend to need a much tighter focus than the leader of a team. For this reason, project managers often must be much more single-minded than team leaders.

Project managers generally can determine their team makeup; team leaders usually must take whoever is assigned to them and often are constrained by company regulations that do not allow them the autonomy to hire and fire their staff. Conversely, a strong project manager has the ability to hire and fire team members—although many project managers seem unaware that they may have this power.

Check with your management to determine what degree of autonomy you have. It has been my observation that most organizations will tolerate a project manager's poaching staff to work on a project, but it is best to confirm this in advance.

Project managers do not have to worry as much as team leaders about upsetting others in the organization. Previously in this book, I made the point that a team leader will have to work hard to avoid the perception that his or her team has formed as an insular, arrogant clique. My suggestion is that team leaders think long and hard before being aggressive about organizational politics. Project managers don't need to be as worried as team leaders about upsetting other people because projects are time-limited.

QUALITIES OF A GOOD PROJECT MANAGER

In Chapter 3, on the topic of team leadership, I identified the top four qualities of a good leader as vision, determination, judgment, and integrity. Although the key qualities of a project manager are similar to those of a team leader, there are differences. The following sections describe the characteristics that a good project manager should possess.

Drive and Determination

In my opinion, drive and determination are among the most important qualities a project manager can have. As stated previously, a team leader's job is to create a credible vision of the future, and to earn the respect and trust of members of his or her team so that they will willingly follow their leader to achieve that vision. The project manager's job is more focused: Deliver the project's objective, on time and within budget. The project manager's determination to deliver, combined with his or her ability to direct the team to achieve the objective, is key to success.

Great project managers often have driven, achievement-oriented personalities. Frequently, their single-mindedness makes them less than nice people to work for. Although I have occasionally worked on projects where great momentum successfully propelled the team to accomplish its objective and we all had fun, such projects are none too common. In the real world, project team members may look back on a successful project with satisfaction, but it is probable that while the project was running, they all complained vociferously about the tyrannical behavior of the project manager. I have observed that few good team leaders are feared by their team; the opposite is true for many successful project managers.

Judgment

Just like a team leader, the project manager will have to make many decisions each and every day. And just like a good team leader, the good project manager must make many good decisions and few bad ones. If you are managing a project and you have poor judgment, *you are in the wrong job.*

Detail

Whereas the good team leader needs a simple, credible vision of the future, the project manager's vision is provided by the project's objective. Project management surely is an area in which the devil is in the detail. To be effective, project managers must have an eye for detail without giving in to the negative practice of micromanaging their team members.

Scheduling

Good project managers seem to perform critical-path analysis in their heads. Although there are software project management tools that help with scheduling complex projects, there is no substitute for a project manager who has an innate feel for scheduling.

Responsibility

A well-run project has an energy and momentum that is palpable. A good project manager cannot afford to let problems fester, but rather must address problems early. There are few circumstances for which benign neglect is a good tactic for a project manager.

In the discussion of team leadership in Chapter 3, I identified qualities, such as judgment, that are essential to doing the job well but that cannot be learned. That having been said, I do believe that although some people definitely are *not* born to be good team leaders, there are many more people who could develop good team leadership skills than realize it. Such people need simply to identify the skills a good team leader must have, and then work on developing those skills. I cannot be so optimistic about project managers: A person either is born to be a great project manager or learns to be a competent project manager, at best. I am particularly sorry to report this because I am one of the people in the latter category. I hope that by analyzing what makes a good project manager, I can help a few more project managers edge toward competency and better.

PROJECT MANAGEMENT STYLES

I have observed three distinct leadership styles of project managers: *the strong manager, the facilitator,* and, strange as the name may sound, *the musical-chairs manager.*

The Strong Manager

No surprises here: The strong project manager is the person who drives his or her team on to success. This leadership style ranges from the dictatorial bully at one extreme, to the hard-but-fair leader at the other. The bullying extreme may evoke fear in subordinates, while the other extreme inspires respect and loyalty with perhaps a touch of fear. One thing that good strong managers share is how they apply the Golden Rule of Management: They usually drive themselves even harder than they drive the rest of the team.

The Facilitator

The facilitator manager is considerably more rare than the strong manager. This kind of leader encourages the team rather than drives it. A facilitator produces a team in which the effort of the team as a single unit is greater than the sum of its parts. Acting as a catalyst to create a team whose members bond and have the common aim of delivering the project's objective, the facilitator more resembles a cheerleader than a dictator. The facilitator tends to quickly develop a consensus with team members on how to solve a problem, rather than unilaterally making all the decisions.

There are two indicators that a team is run by a good facilitator:

- The team is having fun, and has good morale.
- The team has great internal communication.

Project managers who are facilitators usually adopt this style because they find the strong-manager style too brutal. Because a manager chooses facilitation over outright direction does not mean he or she is a weak manager, but the perception of weakness is a danger to be guarded against. Facilitators must make their team confront problems and reach decisions, but if a consensus among team members does not emerge, then the facilitator will have to impose the decision on them.

The Musical–Chairs Manager

Sometimes, a team forms spontaneously to solve a particular problem. In such circumstances, a project team can evolve that will look to different people for leadership in their areas of responsibility. One person may design the solution to the problem; another person might act as the interface to the customer; yet another person may handle administrative matters; and so on, somewhat in the manner of the children's parlor game of Musical Chairs.

Numerous experts laud this style of a project-of-peers as the model organization for projects and, in certain circumstances, I have seen the approach work very well indeed. But often this style leads to disaster. In particular, I believe that the approach does not work when the following difficult conditions exist:

- tight deadlines or budgets
- many unresolved problems for which consensus cannot be reached in a timely fashion
- unidentified or politically charged problems that no one recognizes or wants to face

Despite the praise the project-of-peers, musical-chairs style of management often justifiably receives, I cannot be enthusiastic about it. My distaste for it stems from my stints as a team leader and the frequency with which I have had to impose a project manager on such projects.

PROJECT MANAGEMENT ROLES

Building a team is a bit like creative cooking: A good project manager can put together the same ingredients as a less talented project manager but form a much stronger team. For this reason, I recommend that rather than reading this section as any sort of recipe, just use the information about roles as if it were a set of ingredients with which to work as you build a team.

There are many different roles that may need to be filled in building a successful team, roles that should be considered *before* the project starts. Projects in which some key role is filled by someone without adequate skills are doomed to falter at best, and to fail at worst. Possibly, you may find that you personally are qualified to fill some of the roles, and that other team members also can fill multiple roles. Be prepared to negotiate and renegotiate with your organization to fill any remaining roles that are key to your project's success. Finally, if you do not feel that the project can be staffed to succeed, you may want to consider politely declining the role of manager.

The Design Director

Someone needs to have the overall responsibility for the design of the project's output. If the output is a paper report, then someone needs to be responsible for the key ideas and the report's structure. If the output is a piece of software, then someone needs to be responsible for the software architecture. For the many projects that create a structured object, be it a report, a piece of software, a machine, a building, or some other physical output, someone needs to be responsible for creating and developing the evolving structure throughout the project.

Called the design director or professional/technical lead, this person will also have to resolve any professional or technical disputes relating to design of the product whenever such problems arise during the project.

The Creative Director

Another role that may be important—and that will in some projects be filled by the person who serves as the professional/technical lead—is the creative director. Not all projects will involve a creative role, but the need for creativity extends far beyond the well-recognized creative industries such as architecture and copy-writing. If you need a professional with flair, then your project will probably fail if you have not had the foresight to bring such a person on board.

The Customer Liaison

Delivering something on time and within budget is not enough. What you deliver has to be fit for purpose—that is, the deliverable must meet or, even better, exceed the customer's specifications and expectations. It is not enough for *you* to believe that it is fit for purpose; it is not even enough for it actually to *be* fit for purpose. It is essential that the *customer* thinks that it perfectly satisfies his or her requirements. To ensure that this happens, someone on your team must have responsibility for developing and maintaining open lines of communication and a good relationship with your customer.

What you deliver has to be fit for purpose.

The Marketing Director

On the one hand, you have your customer liaison who can help the team understand what the customer's problems are, how the customer might use the result of the project, and what the customer is likely to value. On the other hand, there are members of the technical and professional staff who know what sorts of things could be delivered and, perhaps equally important, what cannot be delivered. In a general sense, the marketing role matches what can be done to what will be valued.

One of the great challenges in this role is that often customers will not be able to articulate their needs clearly, and it is a creative task to deliver something that they did not really know they wanted until they saw it.

The Salesperson

Some projects may need to be started without a clearly defined set of customers, requiring people on the team to stir up interest among likely prospects. Creating customers where none exist requires a person with drive, highly developed selling skills, and more than an ounce of luck. In some situations, the person who builds the customer base may be the same person who acts as customer liaison, but in the majority of cases, it is better to maintain a distinction between the salesperson and the person who functions as a friend and liaison to customers.

The Project Administrator

The project manager may take on many of the administrative duties of the project, such as overseeing the day-to-day operations, keeping the balance sheet, purchasing supplies, allocating office assignments, and the like. Project administration can also include chasing up and monitoring progress on miscellaneous, non-mainstream activities of the team.

Other Functional Roles

Does the team need someone who writes well? Does the team need access to legal advice? Does the team need someone who has knowledge of a particular type of customer? As project manager, you need to be sure that you have provided for all necessary specialist skills—either hiring specialists as members of the team or contracting with them as independent advisors.

CREATING A BALANCED TEAM

A good project manager will work diligently to fill all necessary roles, but the job is often made more difficult because it is difficult to predict the mix of personalities that will jell to produce a well-balanced team. I cannot give a recipe for creating the mix of personal qualities in a successful team, but I can offer some observations about what ingredients to seek and some to avoid.

A team cannot support many antisocial types. In selecting people to fill key roles, I have sometimes found that the better a person's skill, the more pronounced the antisocial aspects of his or her personality. Abrasive personalities can act as the grit in the oyster that creates the pearl, but a team filled with difficult or antisocial people most likely will break up in discord.

A team needs people who will see a project all the way through to the end. A bad start, such as a failure to create a sound design and a credible implementation plan, can be fatal to a project. Possibly just as disastrous and somewhat more common, however, is the project that has a good start but that loses momentum once the initial rush of enthusiasm dissipates. As project manager, you need to create a core of people who will be sufficiently motivated to see the project through and deliver the finished result.

A team needs one or two catalytic personalities. In the context of a project, catalysts are people whose presence helps create a healthy team. Perhaps the following will not come as news to you, but catalysts are exceedingly good people to have around. The challenge is in identifying them: Look for an elder who can bring a mature, rational perspective to problem-solving or for someone with whom others can share their problems and worries. A catalyst acts as the team's lightning rod, attracting and absorbing worry and anger. When you spot such people, it is worth seeking them out for your next project.

DO'S AND DON'TS

There remain a number of issues that a good project manager needs to address. Some of them require positive action; others require that steps be taken to avoid a particular behavior. Although I've phrased them all in terms of proactive behavior, you will be able to see that there are absolute don'ts to be understood among the do's.

Do clarify your customers' objectives for the project. First and foremost, concentrate on delivering *real value* to your customers. You cannot expect that customers will know precisely what they want at the beginning of a project. One of the prime objectives of any project is for team members to develop a relationship with customers that will result in satisfied and delighted customers at the project's conclusion.

Do clarify your organization's objectives for the project. What will your organization regard as a success and what will it regard as a failure? It is surprising how often a project manager only finds this out after the project has delivered its result; in such cases, it is seldom a pleasant surprise. I have noted that the project's customers may find it difficult to articulate their needs. Likewise, you may discover that your organization will find it difficult to give you clear success and failure criteria. I suggest that you invest as much time as necessary to clarify the project's objectives.

Do seek realistic deadlines. It is very hard to maintain the morale of a project team in the face of an unrealistic deadline. Try to renegotiate such deadlines, but if renegotiation fails, first let management know what time frame you and your team consider realistic for the given deliverable, and then make it clear that despite your reasoned objection to the deadline, you and your team nevertheless will work to try to achieve management's date. Talk with team members to reach agreement with them on what deadline is realistic, so that they know whether they have met your expectations, even though your organization may still cling to an unrealistic target.

Do co-locate team members, either together in one office or as close to each other as possible. Communication within a team falls off dramatically whenever team members are physically separated by more than a few yards. A team that has its own dedicated space is much more likely to jell.

Do encourage social interaction. If team members can eat lunch together, or go out for a drink or bowling after a long day, then it is much more likely that the team will jell.

Do give team members enough time to focus on the project.
Organizations often try to staff a project with people who are already overloaded with work, instructing them to do the project in addition to all their other duties. When staffing a project, you need to insist that team members be given enough time to focus on the project.

SUMMARY

Project management is surprisingly different from managing a team within the structure of an organization. The main reasons for this are that a project usually comes with a well-defined objective and a time limit. As a consequence, the qualities of a good project manager are significantly different from those of a good team leader. Along with numerous other strengths, a good project manager should have the following qualities:

- great drive and determination
- good judgment
- an eye for detail
- a feel for scheduling

Some behavior patterns that are undesirable in a team leader will be acceptable in a project management role. For example, a project manager who exhibits a dictatorial style from time to time probably is not behaving in an inappropriate manner, whereas a team leader cannot afford to behave like a tyrant.

Each of three distinct styles of project management can be successful in the right context:

- the strong manager
- the facilitator
- the musical-chairs manager

Each management style is effective in the proper environment. However, the last style, where there is no single leader, seldom works if there are tight deadlines or contentious issues to resolve.

CHAPTER 6

Managing Different Types of Staff

I can still remember the terror I felt when I was assigned an administrative support person to manage for the first time. As a relatively inexperienced manager, I had been relying on the fact that I was managing people who had similar professional backgrounds to myself, and as a consequence, I could always ask myself, "How would I react to a manager who did that?" I was now responsible for someone whose educational and professional credentials were very different from my own. Should I treat the person any differently from my other staff? Back then, I believed that a manager should treat all staff members the same, but over time I have come to realize that a good manager needs to understand the particular characteristics of different professions and to manage accordingly.

In this chapter, I look at a number of different professions and provide techniques for successfully managing people within them. More detailed discussions of specific professions—such as lawyers and IT software engineers—together with some generic job-type descriptions—such as support, sales, and creative staff—are also presented.

Before getting to the details of the different types of people a front-line manager both must manage and interact with, let's look at some general issues regarding the role experts and professionals may play. These are issues that apply across the board.

EXPERTS AND PROFESSIONALS

When dealing with people in other professions, you, as front-line manager, need to respect their professionalism and expertise. There is absolutely no point in consulting a lawyer, for example, and then refuting or ignoring his or her advice. On the other hand, it does not hurt to keep in mind that professionals do sometimes forget that their principal role is to *support* the manager in making a decision. In many cases, it will be you who has to make the decision on business grounds, and it is the job of your experts to advise you about different possibilities and relevant implications. For example, if a creative person proposes a new product idea, then you will probably have to take the lead in exploring how his or her idea could be adapted to bring it to market; you will pose market scenarios, but the creative person will be the one who knows best how to adapt the idea to those scenarios.

Interacting with people whose expertise is in a different area from your own is a bit of an art, but there are many useful ways to behave that can help you with your interactions. The following paragraphs describe some of these behavioral strategies.

Never show disrespect for an expert's professionalism. Many experts can try the patience of a saint. No matter how annoyed you feel, never allow your annoyance to be expressed in a disrespectful manner. For many experts, the worst of all insults is to have their ability to perform their job questioned.

Do not allow yourself to be sidetracked by jargon. People who are truly competent *can* make themselves understood to laymen without relying on the jargon that clutters most specialized industries. Experts who hide behind a veneer of "professional mystique" may be more intent on intimidating you than on enlightening you. It is not only acceptable, but also essential, that you require your experts to explain their points to you in language that you can understand. If this means asking question after question after question, so be it. The expert will eventually get the message that you insist on understanding the issues that are relevant to the decisions you have to make.

Never show disrespect for an expert's professionalism.

Explain your problems to your experts. I have found that it is nearly always productive to explain your problem area to an expert who is advising you. To help you, the specialist needs to understand the nature of the problems you face, and it is likely that you will discover that many experts are fascinated to find out how your business works. However, remember not to use jargon with them!

Beware of advocacy. Experts sometimes have a nasty habit of holding strong, and not entirely rational, views on certain topics within their area of expertise. If ever you detect the gleam of religious fervor in your adviser's eyes, be on guard and seek a second opinion.

Beware of the trendy solution. Another nasty habit among certain professionals is to follow the latest fad. You only need look at your own area of management to see how many managers slavishly adopt the latest quack nostrum peddled by some management guru. If you suspect this to be the case, ask how well established the particular technique is, and ask for examples of the successful use of the solution proposed.

Be suspicious when told something is impossible. Experts will seldom tell an outright lie, but when an expert says that something is impossible, he or she may know that if the question or request were changed slightly, it would no longer be impossible to achieve. Explore the underlying issues, being careful not to let the experts bury you in irrelevant detail, and ask, "Is there anything I can do that will give me what I want?" If the answer is negative, next ask, "What can I do to get eighty percent of what I want?" and so on.

Beware of self-serving advice. I have done a fair amount of management consulting in my career and know how difficult it is to resist the temptation to recommend an issue for further study. Since the additional work probably would be performed by the expert who recommended it, the advice is surely suspect. Experts who want you to become dependent on their advice should be shown the door. Given human nature, you must take the lead in ensuring that you get the advice that is *best for you,* not best for your advisers.

Beware of advisers withholding relevant information from you. Some experts seem to work on the basis that knowledge is power, and will attempt to ration the information they give you.

Make sure you have the right expert. No one would be willing to undergo open-heart surgery performed by an oncologist, but it is very common for people to underestimate the levels of specialization needed in other professions. My brother told me about the approach he used to resolve a difficult employment problem he had with his employer—he hired an employment-law specialist to stand up against the general-law advisers used by his employer. He won . . . easily! As another example, would you want a large IT database project being led by someone doing a large database implementation for the first time? Make sure your adviser has the necessary specialist knowledge.

Although the preceding paragraphs demonstrate how careful you must be when dealing with experts, the way to get the best from your advisers is to *keep asking questions until you fully understand the issues*. Use your advisers to inform you of all relevant issues, but make it clear that you will make the decisions, not them.

LOOKING AT STEREOTYPES

In the sections that follow, you may feel that I am guilty of perpetuating offensive stereotypes about different professions. Please keep in mind as you read that, in my own career, I have at various times been a creative type, an IT person, a salesman, and also a consultant; so if I insult such people, I also insult myself. I will try to avoid being offensive, but it is my view that many professionals do indeed exhibit stereotypical characteristics. I am not saying that every member of every profession displays the qualities I describe, but different professions do tend to act, and react, in particular ways. Managers can benefit from being aware of how and why different professions act the way they do.

Lawyers

I have a confession to make: The subject of law fascinates me, and I have enjoyed my interactions with legal experts and contracts staff throughout the years I have been in management. So, let me start this section on stereotypes by giving the lawyers' side of the story.

From the lawyer's viewpoint

First, to hear a lawyer tell it, people always wait until it's too late to consult their attorney: If only people asked for advice in good time, then life would be so much easier. Second, no one remembers the pressure the lawyer was put under to get a contract out quickly, when years later the agreement is tested in court and found to be poorly drafted. Third, people do not understand the importance of legal issues and treat the lawyer as an irritating nuisance who keeps them from getting on with their business, rather than as an expert who is trying to stop the careless manager from unnecessarily risking the business. Fourth, . . .

Because I am an essentially humane sort, I will spare you Clauses 4 through 332 of the "Lament of the Lawyer," but trust that you can find at least some truth in the three laments I have listed. The fact is, a frosty relationship often exists between the

113

manager or businessman and the lawyer. The reason for this is that the fundamental personality traits of managers and lawyers tend to be diametrically opposed.

Managers tend to be risk-takers, while lawyers are trained to be risk-averse. I believe that managers and lawyers should openly acknowledge this fundamental divide and try to appreciate the views of the other side. The middle ground is *risk-management*—your lawyer must ensure that you understand the full implications of all the risks you choose to accept.

An additional personality issue of which managers need to be aware is that *legal training reinforces adversarial personalities*. Lawyers are trained to win arguments, and most good lawyers enjoy a good fight. The fact that a good fight is usually highly profitable for lawyers enters into the equation as well.

From the manager's viewpoint

Looking at lawyers and the law from the specific perspective of the front-line manager helps us to identify some behavior and practices that the manager can use to his or her advantage:

Lawyers cannot give short answers to questions. I have noticed that when lawyers answer a question, they frequently give a very full context to their answer, sometimes going all the way back to first principles. It is my experience that it is hopeless to resist, and it is much better to listen patiently—you may even learn something new.

Lawyers cannot give short answers to questions.

Lawyers should not be the key decision-makers in the early stages of business negotiations. The purpose of a legal agreement is to accurately record a deal that has been negotiated by business people. Lawyers generally do not have the right motivations, or the right temperaments, for business negotiations.

Lawyers should be encouraged to create contracts like prenuptials. One of the main services that lawyers provide is to help parties to a contract agree to the terms while the parties are still friends, much like an engaged couple agrees to a prenuptial agreement that will determine property and custodial rights in the event of a divorce. If you can get contracts drafted to resemble prenuptials, you will have done yourself a big service.

Lawyers should not be permitted to delay urgent action. Of all the times I have found lawyers to be unhelpful, the most extreme is when there is a crisis. Lawyers, by their nature and training, like to fully research a topic before offering advice; as a result, they react badly to having to give the immediate advice needed in a crisis. A second major problem with how lawyers respond in times of crisis is that the difficulty can often be best resolved from a public-relations perspective, by an honest admission of responsibility. Lawyers hate to have their clients admit liability and, consequently, a strong business lead may be necessary to put the lawyers "back in the box." Once the lawyers realize that you really do intend to apologize, they will be of great use in drafting a positive PR response while still insuring that liability is minimized.

IT Staff

Unlike with lawyers, problems in dealing with IT staff have more to do with the nature of the IT profession than with the particular personality traits of staff members. Although IT professionals use the phrase *software engineering*, the front-line manager needs to understand that software engineering is not an engineering discipline in the same way that civil engineering is. To state that software is based on discrete mathematics while other sorts of engineering are based on continuous mathematics probably would not explain much, so I will use an illustrative example. To test a civil engineering design, there are numerous techniques available; for example, one can build a scale model of a bridge design and then test it for stresses in a wind tunnel, or one can use computer models to test the design. These techniques depend on continuous mathematics. To exhaustively test anything but the simplest of computer programs takes far too much time to be practical. To use mathematics to prove the correctness of anything but the simplest of programs is beyond current technology. The following effects of this mathematical "problem" are well known:

- Even the best software programs contain bugs.
- Software projects are prone to disastrous cost and time overruns.

There are a number of issues that managers need to address when dealing with IT staff and IT projects, as discussed below.

Software estimation

Most IT staff members are incurable optimists when it comes to estimating how much time and money a piece of software will take to complete. Given the mathematical complexity underlying software, it is not surprising that there are no reliable techniques for software estimation. As a manager, you need to know the truth: The only technique that works reasonably well is by analogy—that is, by comparing the current project with a past project. Comparing a project with the nearest similar project in size, complexity, and functionality can give you a rough idea of time and cost. Yet the accuracy of even this technique can easily be undermined by the differences between the new and the old project—for example, differences such as staff abilities, or a piece of functionality that proves very hard to implement. If you cannot find a good analogy, then your project faces a major risk of time and cost overruns; even with a good analogy, the risks are never small. In summary,

Be afraid; be very afraid.

A few additional hints:

- Any product vendor selling you any technique or tool that makes software development highly predictable is a liar (but the product may be worth buying anyway).
- Quality systems do not solve this problem (but they may be worth using anyway).
- Project management processes cannot solve this problem (but they may highlight the severity of the problem earlier).

Now for a helpful comment:

A third of the way through a software project, the staff on the project will have a very good idea of how long the entire project will take, but the estimate will still be too optimistic.

This begs the question, How much contingency should the manager add at this stage to get an accurate estimate? The best I can do is offer an observation, which is that when a software engineer says that the project is 80 percent complete, it is at most only 50 percent done. In practice, I tend to add about 30 percent to the estimates I get from staff members when they are a third of the way through the time originally allotted for a project.

Although it is seldom easy, you must plan to review the deadlines and cost estimates about a third of the way through the project. IT staff members, just like most people, become demoralized when they know they are working to impossible deadlines.

Software project failures

Software projects usually fail for any of a few well-known reasons, as listed below. Because you, as the manager, have responsibility for most of them, they probably will seem very familiar:

- *The requirement for the software is much too ambitious.* It is your duty to ensure that the team sticks to the KISS principle: Keep It Simple, Stupid! IT staff members tend to love their technology and will seldom question the need for more and more computerization.

Keep It Simple, Stupid!

- *The requirement for the software becomes divorced from the needs of its ultimate users.*
- *The management is weak.* Managers who do not intervene when software-related problems arise or who refuse to make important decisions because they do not feel qualified to make judgments about a software project are responsible for project failure, a topic I will discuss in more detail later in this section.
- *Unrealistic deadlines are accepted, and senior management is not properly briefed on the underlying problems.*
- *Consultants are overly relied on.*

- *Staff members work to re-invent the wheel, rather than use off-the-shelf packages (and occasionally vice versa).*
- *Risks posed by suppliers and subcontractors are poorly handled.*
- *New software is introduced using the big-bang method.* It is always wise to run a new system in parallel with any system being replaced. Ensure that there is a fallback mode of operation for when the new software falls in a fiery heap—because chances are good that it will!

Having started this section by stating that software engineering is very different from other engineering disciplines, the truth is that most of the reasons projects fail apply equally to any technical job.

Software versions

Most good software engineers know that they need to rip up their software at least twice in the process of developing any substantial piece of code. Most know that it's the third version of software that works. Usually, software engineers have to hide the fact from their managers that they have thrown away most of the original software code. Hopefully, by my explaining this truth, I'll have helped each and every one of you front-line managers to actively plan for the inevitable rewrites and to gain the respect of your IT staff in the process. If you find that your IT staff does not feel that the software would benefit from a rewrite, you need to start worrying about the quality of your IT staff.

Security

Every profession seems to have its no-win situations, and security seems to be the biggest no-win situation IT staff members face. Businesses are loath to invest in proper IT security, but are quick to shoot the IT experts when security is breached. Please listen carefully when members of your IT staff discuss security issues.

IT project management

Although you may know little or nothing about how to write software, your expertise, judgment, and leadership are vital in a number of areas.

Ensure that the functional specification of the software is appropriate to the needs of your business. It is well known that many of the problems in software projects stem from mistakes made in identifying the requirements for the software. I have already mentioned the importance of KISS, but let me emphasize the point again: You must constantly battle against complexity in the software's functional specification. You must also ensure that the specification of the software meets the requirements of your business. Whether the software is for internal use or external sale, it is a means to an end, not an end in itself. You must champion the role of the software users, whether they are staff within your organization or your external customers' staff. In addition to this role in determining the functional specification, you have an even greater responsibility in ensuring that the nonfunctional characteristics of the software meet the needs of your business, as I will discuss in the next section.

Ensure that the architecture of the software has the properties your business needs. How easy is it to modify the functionality of the software? How easy is it to port the software to a different operating system? How easy is it to interface the software to other pieces of software on the same or different computers? How easy is it for customers to customize the software? How easy is it to scale the software so that it can handle more users or more data?

Depending on the purpose of the software, some or all of these questions may be very relevant—so ask them! It is important for managers to realize that none of the desirable *-ilities* (portability, flexibility, scalability, and so on) will happen by accident; they occur because the software was designed specifically to provide such properties. IT staff members tend to focus on delivering an initial capability and often pay too little attention to how the software will become a long-term part of the business. The way the software is structured (its architecture) will determine the answers to the questions I have posed. As front-line manager, you should never need to know about the detailed lines of code within a software system, but you need to ask the right questions to ensure that the architecture is appropriate to your business needs.

Be flexible in adapting business processes to better suit off-the-shelf software. This point may appear to contradict the previous point. The truth is that many off-the-shelf packages impose severe constraints on the business processes they support. This means that if you want to maximize the savings from using off-the-shelf software, you have to be willing to accept the constraints that that software imposes on your business requirements.

Ensure that appropriate development processes are put in place. What development processes am I thinking about? I am principally referring to the things that IT staff members typically know they do badly, such as in the following areas:

- testing
- documentation
- coding standards
- code reviews

It has been my experience that the greatest problem area of these is testing. I strongly advise that you find out early in a project what the test plan is, and ensure that there is adequate time and sufficient resources to do it properly. While all competent IT staff members will want to test their own code, there is no substitute for energetic, independent software testing.

Creative Types

Somewhat akin to herding cats, managing creative types rarely is easy. Words such as arrogant, petulant, insecure, socially inept, unconventional, and prima donna spring to my mind when I begin describing the personality traits of creative people, but let's look beyond the stereotypes to see what makes creative people tick, and to see what management techniques can be successfully deployed on such staff.

Fear

Most creative people do not know how they "do it." As a consequence, most creative people worry, or to be more precise, are terrified, that their creative ability will desert them. (As I sit typing this paragraph, I worry that writer's block is waiting to strike down my muse.) How do you manage this fear in your creative staff? The first thing to do is to create a culture that gives creative people a feeling of security. Handle creative staff members sensitively when their creativity temporarily deserts them, and try some of the following well-proven techniques:

- Reassure the person that a temporary loss of creativity is a perfectly normal situation.
- Remove the pressure of deadlines.
- Keep the person very busy on routine work; the busier a person is, the more likely he or she is to regain creativity.

Obsession

Many creative people need to become totally obsessed by a task in order to be creative. Such obsession can lead to poor relations between creative staff and the rest of your team. If you manage to stop them from being obsessive, they may lose their creativity. If the obsession is detrimental to productivity, you will need to manage the effects that the obsession causes—but keep in mind that you probably cannot remove the root cause of the obsession. It is important to distinguish the problems that are an inherent part of creativity (which you can do little or nothing about) from those that just happen to be related to creativity (which you can tackle).

Creativity often requires obsession.

Rule-breaking

Many creative types believe that the rules don't apply to them, but oh yes, they do! Thinking that the rules don't apply is one of the traits related to creativity that you can tackle. I would recommend that you be a bit tolerant of creative staff not sticking to the rules. For example, I have refrained from formally disciplining creative staff when I might have started disciplinary proceedings against a less creative staff member, because obsession does make creative staff more forgetful. However, in the final analysis, there is no reason why creative people should be allowed to get away with not obeying departmental rules and processes like filling in their time sheets or notifying people when they will be out of the office. A related, but subtly different problem pertains to eccentric individuality.

Eccentricity

In many areas such as dress, behavior, and personal hygiene, creative people stray well outside the norms expected of staff. As long as the degree of individuality is not offensive to other staff, I would recommend that you be as tolerant as the health

123

department or your organization allows. Having to ask a staff member to wash more frequently is definitely one of the more unpleasant tasks that you as a manager may have to face, but you do have to face it.

In areas such as personal hygiene,
creative people stray well outside the norms.

Lethargy

People on the creative staff often suffer from a form of torpor before they embark on a creative task. This is perfectly normal, and there is no harm in gently cajoling creative staff to try starting the task.

Sensitivity to surroundings

Creative people usually need to achieve an almost trance-like state of concentration, which psychologists refer to as "flow." External distractions can easily prevent the attainment of flow. For this reason, creativity and open-plan offices tend to be incompatible. For some creative staff, listening to music on headphones can help, but if open office space is an issue for your staff, *you* may need to be creative in your management approach. Allowing creative people to work from home or in isolated study rooms may be the answer. Alternatively, you may need to reorganize your open-plan accommodations so that those needing quiet are located close together.

Paranoia

Not all creative people exhibit paranoid behavior and think that everyone is out to get them, but it appears to me that paranoia is more common among creative people than in the employed population as a whole. Paranoid types need regular desensitizing, which the manager can handle by talking out their irrational fears with them. However, people who truly suffer from paranoia need professional help.

Appreciation

It is important to recognize the fact that many creative people excessively crave appreciation; if you fail to give praise as deserved, you risk de-motivating a creative staff member. It is also important to understand the role appreciation can play, because expressing it can provide valuable opportunities for managing creative staff. Sometimes, flattery *will* get you what you want. A creative person's need for appreciation can help you sell him or her on a job, because a task with a high profile, if performed well, will garner a lot of credit.

Consultants

In the preceding sections of this chapter, I have not felt the need to define my terms, principally because I think that the picture in my head of, say, a lawyer or IT staff member is likely to accord with the reader's. There is, however, a very narrow dividing line between consultants and some subcontractors, making it necessary for me to be precise. In this section, I regard a consultant to be someone who gives advice, not someone who rolls up his or her sleeves to do the "real work." Admittedly, this definition points to one of the negative perceptions about consultants, calling to mind the saying, "Those who can, do, those who can't, teach." In my field, the saying often is rephrased as, "Those who can, do, those who can't, consult." The perception that consultants give advice because they can't actually do the work is a sensitive issue with many consultants, but it has been my experience that it tends to be the best consultants who worry most about this aspect of their work.

It is worth being aware of the potential sensitivity about this issue for consultants, because you mention it to a consultant at your peril.

Personality traits

There are a number of strong characteristics that most consultants share. Understanding these traits will help you manage consultants, enabling you to get the best out of them. In the paragraphs that follow, I discuss the traits—both positive and negative—and share my views regarding interactions you may have with two different types of consultants; specifically, the consultants you or your organization hire to advise you, and the staff members you contract out as consultants to your customers. I'll emphasize the negatives, but there are plenty of good consultants out there in the world. Trust me!

Consultants tend to have the mentality of mercenaries. It is important that you not forget that consultants are hired guns. You can buy their professionalism, but you seldom can buy their loyalty. A consequence of this is that consultants you hire need to be very tightly managed. You may manage your own staff members in a hands-off manner because of their loyalty to the team and the organization or because of their ownership of the team culture, but you will do best if you explicitly set the parameters within which consultants work.

If, on the other hand, your business is *selling* consultancy rather than hiring it, then you need to be aware that the hired-gun mentality does not naturally produce team players, and that many consultants are essentially loners who may well put their own interests above the interests of the team. This sounds like a terminal condition, but I have found one excellent way to create loyalty from consultants: Most consultants fear that the organization they work for will milk them for the maximum revenue that their current knowledge can generate, and then will spit them out when their expertise becomes outdated. If you can offer the consultants on your team the chance to acquire new skills, it is much more likely that they will remain loyal to you and your team.

Consultants tend to exhibit competitive, often intolerant, personalities. The highly rigorous and competitive academic and professional training most professionals have undergone by the time they are employed as consultants contributes significantly to heightening their competitive nature, often giving them an inflated view of their own importance. Management consultants, in particular, are expected to have earned MBAs, preferably in programs that are modeled on the MBA course structure at Harvard University. In addition, many management consulting companies have cultures that in some way replicate the highly competitive culture pioneered at McKinsey & Company, the international firm regarded by many as the father of all modern management consulting companies.

Fueled by the competitive nature of their consulting firms, many consultants work excessively long hours, under extreme pressure—conditions that can contribute to inflaming an already difficult personality. Although it would be too strong a generalization to say that all consultants are overly competitive and view themselves as professionally superior to others, competitiveness and intolerance are sufficiently marked traits to merit a manager's awareness. As their manager, you will need to set clear limits that define acceptable behavior, and take appropriate action when a consultant exceeds those limits.

Consultants tend to overplay remuneration. Consultancy is one of the best-paid professions. Unfortunately, the high pay scale operates in tandem with negative traits such as competitiveness and weak team-playing skills to produce consultants who focus excessively on the amount of money they personally earn. There is almost no way a manager of consultants can avoid being sucked into highly aggressive salary negotiations, and few of the techniques that can be applied to other staff

127

members to moderate their salary aspirations will work. An inflated pay scale is one of the reasons why staff turnover among consultants is so high, and is the main reason why consulting is one of the few professions in which top staff members may earn salaries similar to what a headhunter or poacher would pay to lure them to a competing firm.

One technique that is worth considering is the use of nonmonetary rewards. The presence of perks and visible signs of status can dissuade a poacher from matching what a consultant already enjoys, for fear of opening the floodgates to dissatisfaction among the poacher's current stable of recruited consultants. This non-salary-based form of remuneration can give you a powerful argument for persuading your consultants to stay with you.

Consultants tend to intellectualize rather than empathize. Consultants typically are analytical people who pride themselves on being able to understand complex problems and envision solutions. Following the advice of a consultant who has been hired from the outside to solve such problems can cause pain and grief to some members of your existing staff. Whenever outside consultants disregard the pain their advice might cause, serious tensions can arise between them and the staff members who work within the organizations they are advising.

Professional (and unprofessional) behavior

The preceding paragraphs address common *personality* traits typical of consultants. The following paragraphs look at problematical *professional* behavior that a front-line manager will need to anticipate.

Many consultants have strong but unusual ethics. As I approach this issue of ethics, I am reminded of an anecdote about a burglar who regarded himself as being a cut above the "average" because he never vandalized the houses he robbed and he never carried a weapon. Although he was a petty thief, the burglar believed himself to be ethical. I see similarity in the behavior of consultants who are under strong business pressures to function in ways that do not display the highest levels of integrity. They believe themselves to be ethical, but blame their behavior on the demands of their job.

Although most consultants give in, at least partially, to business demands and pressures, this behavior does not mean that they do not have a strong sense of ethics—it's just that you, as a front-line manager, may find it difficult to understand their particular brand of ethics. It is especially important for you to acknowledge this disparate viewpoint because recognizing it can prepare you for the negative and often emotional reaction you may receive if you ask a consultant to do something that he or she regards as unethical. If you encounter a consultant becoming emotional, it may well be that you unwittingly have brushed up against an area of that consultant's ethics that you should probe for the underlying motivation.

Many consultants tell you what you want to hear. Telling the customer what he or she wants to hear is the oldest trick in the consulting book. The only reason I include such a well-known ploy in this chapter is that I see it repeated time and time again—be forewarned.

Many consultants tell you what you want to hear.

Many consultants prefer to tell good news rather than bad.
Related to the previous point, good news is what most people
prefer to hear. Imagine a situation in which a marketing consultant is brought in to advise a customer on the marketing of a
particular product and finds that the product is almost bound
to fail to be profitable. What do you think are the chances that
the consultant tells the client that the product is a likely dud?
This situation occurs in many insidious ways, with consultants
glossing over fundamental problems they think their customers do not wish to acknowledge.

*Many consultants want customers to become dependent on
them.* It is very easy for one consultancy contract to lead seam-
lessly into the next. You cannot expect consultants to tell you
that their advice is no longer needed; it is your responsibility to
decide when paying for a consultant's advice is no longer cost-
effective.

Many consultants favor one-size-fits-all advice. Consultancies sometimes seek to maximize their profitability by making their service a commodity. They do this by addressing a
particular range of problems, and training their consultants to
pigeonhole the customer's problem into one of a limited number of problem types, each of which has a standard solution.
By doing this, they can facilitate a consultant's job by training
him or her using a standardized method. They can also
increase their consultants' productivity by producing reports
that contain large amounts of pre-written material. It is your
job as front-line manager to ensure that your consultants give
advice that is fully relevant to your particular situation. If you
are unsure that a consultant could recognize the uniqueness of
a particular situation, it is worth considering dispensing with
his or her services.

Many consultants promote trendy methodologies. Another
approach favored by some consultancies is to offer a *commod-
ity-oriented service* that is based on some trendy methodology.
In such a situation, any limitations in the method (and, in my
opinion, *all* methods have limitations) can lead to inaccurate
advice. The best consultancy comes from the best consultants;

if you have bought the services of a well-trained monkey, then you only have yourself to blame.

Many consultants employ bait-and-switch tactics. Given the two preceding points about how consultancy firms tailor their services to maximize profitability, you may not be surprised to learn that the bait-and-switch technique is widespread in the consultancy business. The approach, which involves using the best consultants to win a contract and then second-rate consultants to service the contract, is evident in every business sector, but it clearly is not a practice you'll want to encourage!

Having given consultants a pretty good scalding in this section, I would like to close with a few words in their defense. As a consultant myself, I can report firsthand that there is nothing more depressing than working for a client who has brought consultants in just to justify what the client wanted to do anyway. In particular, being brought in to recommend staff cuts has to be one of the most soul-wrenching jobs in the world. The converse, working for clients who genuinely want insight into their problems, is a delight. In short, clients get the consultants they deserve; perhaps it also can be said that consultants get the clients they deserve.

Sales Staff

For many front-line managers, salespeople, like consultants, frequently can be invaluable, but more often are a necessary evil. As the saying goes, you can't live with them, and you can't live without them. One reason for this paradox is that salespeople and consultants exhibit many of the same personality and behavioral characteristics. Although there are exceptions to every generalization, both salespeople and consultants tend to be poor team players, to be motivated by money, to be highly competitive, to indulge driven personalities, and to allow integrity to take a backseat. Their work habits are also similar: They both tend to work very long hours. Characteristics such as those shared by salespeople and consultants are not negative in and of themselves—in the right hands, each of these traits and habits can be cultivated to become a strength—but, in my experience, such positive cultivation rarely occurs unless the front-line manager takes an aggressively proactive stance.

Typically, there is an observable difference between consultants and salespeople: Consultants tend to be highly analytical and rational, whereas salespeople frequently appear to be quite the opposite. By being aware of the distinguishing characteristics of salespeople, including those discussed in the following paragraphs, the front-line manager may be able to turn potentially negative traits into attributes.

Salespeople may be merciless hunters. Top salespeople enjoy chasing their quarry, and delight in going for the kill. Once they have begun to stalk their prey, they may find it hard to abandon the hunt. It is important to recognize this quality if you manage salespeople, because many will be willing to go to unacceptable lengths to clinch a deal. The sorts of problems that an overly zealous salesperson may create include

- offering too large a discount
- making unrealistic promises, such as an impossible-to-meet delivery date
- offering too many, or impossible, changes to the standard product
- offering too many sweeteners, such as free consulting services
- overselling product or service capabilities

It is your job as manager to set the precise parameters under which your salespeople operate, and to exercise discipline when (*not if*) those parameters are breached.

Salespeople may be unsatisfactory team players. Not infrequently, salespeople have antagonistic relationships with product-development and customer-service staff. Many salespeople feel, sometimes with justification, that they understand the customer better than "the boys in the back room" possibly could; that their views on how the product or service should be developed to make it more salable are not properly recognized; that they are the front line of the organization and everyone else should realize that they are only there to support sales; and that the rest of the organization fails to display a proper can-do attitude.

The antagonism stems principally from the fact that base-staff members may harbor a host of complaints, including that salespeople do not understand the complexity and profession-alism needed to deliver a quality product or service; that sales-people ask staff to meet impossible deadlines or to compromise the quality of the product or service; that salespeople do not understand the nature of the product or service and request features inconsistent with product or service ethos; that sales-people try to keep them away from the customers; and, most irritating of all, that salespeople earn bonuses as a result of work done by base-staff members themselves.

As a front-line manager, you need to recognize what causes the antagonism and work to smooth the interface between sales and base staff. Whether the salespeople you manage naturally are team players or artfully must be molded to function as part of a team, do everything possible to ensure the highest level of cooperation among those you manage.

Salespeople may be too quick to blame others. Why sales-people seem neurotically eager to blame problems on others probably can only be determined through years of psycho-analysis—either for them or for the front-line manager—but from what I have observed, blaming others is a very marked behavioral trait in salespeople. As manager, you know to always get the facts, but be particularly careful to get *all* the facts before you judge who's to blame when salespeople are involved.

Salespeople may expect to work in a bonus culture. If you are a manager who thinks that bonuses are a crude way to motivate staff and you use them sparingly, keep in mind that, in many organizations, bonuses are the *norm* for motivating salespeople. As with all conditions of enterprise—whether the business involves staff members or consultants or subcontractors—it is essential that you set the parameters for bonuses carefully. As noted in Chapter 1, if a bonus is predicated on volume of business, then salespeople may not be motivated to push for the highest possible price. If bonuses are unavoidable, it is usually wise to base them on margins and volume.

Support Staff

If you can honestly state that, as a front-line manager, you treat administrative and support staff in exactly the same way as all other team members, then award yourself a gold star for good management and skip this section. The fact is, many managers find it difficult to manage staff whose educational and professional backgrounds are very different from their own. In many settings, support and administrative staff members will have received a lower level of formal education than others on the team, but their dedication and commitment to the job can get them further in a team setting than many people with more advanced degrees. However, if, like me, you find disparate academic and professional qualifications difficult to manage, I offer the following pointers about qualities to look for in support staff.

Support staff must have common sense. Sometimes, the most academically qualified people have the least common sense. In support staff, look first for common sense and enthusiasm; look last at academic credentials.

Support staff must be highly reliable. The key to good support is its reliability. It is not acceptable if team members feel that they have to constantly check up on support staff, rather than trusting them to get on with it.

Support staff must be open to direction and accessible to team members. Support staff members are on the team to help other people do their jobs, but do not expect that your team members will naturally know how to use the support to best effect. In order to get the most out of the whole team as a unified entity, dispel lingering misconceptions, such as the following shockingly common ones:

- All support staff members are incompetents and idiots.
- All support staff members are as knowledgeable as the people they support.
- All support staff members are mind readers.
- All support staff members are too busy to help individuals on the team.

The final misconception that must be dispelled is one that cannot be harbored by anyone you manage, whether support staff or otherwise. The most dangerous conviction anyone on a team can have is, *my job is the most urgent one.*

The knack in managing support staff is knowing how much detail and background information you need to give a particular person, and whether it needs to be in written form or can be communicated verbally. Some support staff members can work with a less-than-precise specification, while others will need a fair amount of detail. Let support staff members know deadlines for each piece of work, and clarify what priority the work has in relation to their other tasks.

Support staff must be receptive to job-specific training. Many support staff members have never been told how to provide good customer service to those they support. For example, they may never have been taught the importance of giving people feedback on the progress of a task or of warning them in good time of any likely delays. As manager, you must make it clear that investing in the training of support staff can pay great dividends—and then you must act according to your belief by properly training people to do the job. In particular, invest in keeping your support staff's skills current in the use of computing technology.

Support staff deserve to be shown respect. Some people may try to treat support staff members like servants, but let your team know that such behavior is unacceptable. Although all staff members must behave in a way that merits their teammates' courtesy and consideration, support staff members especially are to be shown respect—both as individuals and as contributors to the team.

Sad to say, respect among team members does not always happen under pressure of deadline. I once went so far as to order individuals on my team's support staff to report the names of discourteous staff to me. I then made it clear to rude staff members that unless they mended their ways, they would have support withdrawn from them. Politeness does not mean that the team should tolerate sloppy service, however. If support is not totally reliable, then those responsible for providing it should be politely, but firmly, made aware that they let a team member down.

SUMMARY

Hear what your experts are telling you. Insist that issues be explained to you in a way that you can understand. Keep asking questions until you do understand.

Beware of experts or professionals who

- advocate particular solutions
- say that something is impossible
- seek to make you dependent on their continued advice

When dealing with lawyers, remember that they tend to be risk-averse, hate moving quickly, and like a good argument (preferably in court).

When dealing with IT staff, remember that software engineering is not a traditional engineering discipline. Estimating software projects is a blind art, largely based on comparison with past projects. One useful technique is to redo your estimates about a third of the way through the project.

Most software projects fail for reasons that are within management's control:

- inadequate requirements
- poor consideration of the users' view of the software
- too much complexity in the software's specification

- unrealistic deadlines
- unwillingness to confront problems

Other key roles associated with managing software projects include

- ensuring that nonfunctional software properties are addressed by the system architecture
- ensuring that there are adequate processes for testing, code management, documentation, coding standards, and code reviews

When dealing with creative types, remember that many of them fear the loss of their creativity and will need continuous reassurance. Creative people often have to be obsessive in order to be creative, and you will need to decide how tolerant you will be of their obsessions and other unattractive behavioral traits.

Consultants tend to have a hired-gun mentality. Many will not be team players; others will be very self-centered and focused on money.

Salespeople have many of the same characteristics as consultants. You need to remember that they are like hunters, and are accustomed to a culture in which financial bonuses are the norm. Because salespeople probably will react very crudely to any financial incentives you establish, set them very carefully.

Insist that support staff members be highly reliable in the service they provide. Remember that a lack of formal education does not imply a lack of common sense, and pay particular attention to training. You may need to train your team in how to get the best out of the support staff, but you also must invest in training support-staff personnel to keep them current.

CHAPTER 7

Managing
Team Culture

One sure sign that you are getting it right as a manager is when your team behaves the way you want it to behave—without being supervised or explicitly instructed to do so. By establishing a strongly defined culture within the team, you can be fairly certain of achieving this desirable state. Team members who instinctively know "this is the way we do things" and "we don't do things like that," will tend to act in ways you approve of, and will avoid doing things you would not condone. Even better, peer pressure within the team will encourage everyone to behave in accord with the team culture.

Another desirable consequence of allowing the team culture to reinforce your own standards and principles is that team members will be able to easily predict how you would react to a particular set of circumstances. Hearing someone say "I knew you would want it done that way" should be taken as a compliment of the highest order.

So how do you achieve a good, strong culture? Rephrasing the Golden Rule of Management gives a guideline:

Consistent behavior by the leader sets the tone for the culture.

Consistency is the key—inconsistent behavior will very rapidly produce a dysfunctional culture. You should constantly monitor your own physical reactions in order to eliminate the possi-

138

bility of conveying a conflicting message. Similarly, if your words are inconsistent with your actions, then your actions will set the culture but the inconsistency will undermine your personal standing.

It is nearly impossible to overstate how strongly the Golden Rule of Management applies to the factors that go into creating a team culture. Without your even being conscious of what is happening, you may find that your team's culture will take on aspects of your own personality—to the degree that it becomes quite spooky. To avoid unnecessary litigation, I will refrain from pointing out some of the more obvious examples, but if you think about companies with conspicuously well-known chief executives, you will notice that many have a culture that reflects the personality traits of their leaders.

UNDERSTAND THE EXISTING CULTURE

Chances are, you took over leadership of an existing team. If so, you need to understand what culture you have inherited, and in particular what aspects of the culture are highly valued by your staff. Changing any aspect of the existing culture will need skillful and honest handling. Generally speaking, a wise new manager takes time to understand a new team and avoids hasty changes of direction.

A second influence on your team's culture will be if your organization has strong cultural traits. For example, if you work for an aggressive and combative organization, you will have difficulty if you try to create a culture that runs directly counter to this organizational bias.

In the next two sections of this chapter, I discuss different kinds of culture, and the techniques you can use to create the specific culture that you want.

WHAT TEAM CULTURE DO *YOU* WANT?

Most probably, you will want to foster a team culture that is change- and customer-oriented, principled, and sensitive to individual preferences. Before reading further, however, you might try the following: Based on your experience prior to becoming a manager, list the qualities you value most in a corporate culture and then list those characteristics you want to avoid. The qualities you admire may include those described in the paragraphs that follow, but don't be surprised if your list differs—the culture you foster should be unique to you.

A customer-oriented culture

As a front-line manager functioning at what probably is one of the lower levels of management, you—and members of your team—undoubtedly will deal with customers within or outside the organization. If this is the case, you need to have strong cultural values about customer service, and you need to articulate those values to be implemented by your team.

An outward-looking culture

One aspect of a customer-oriented culture is that it tends to be outward-looking rather than introspective. An outward-looking culture will be led by someone whose main interest is the value of the team's outputs, and who thinks that the internal processes of the team are just a means to an end, rather than an end in themselves.

A culture of selected extremes

That most strong cultures have extreme aspects to them is a commonly held view, leading people to believe that including extreme characteristics—such as working very long hours, providing heroic customer service, or being hyper-competitive— will guarantee a strong culture. A culture is a complex, social system, and any soft science that grows up around such complex systems—be it management science, psychology, or economics—is prone to incorrect suppositions of cause and effect. The fact that strong cultures often possess extreme characteristics does not mean that you can make a culture strong by making it extreme. Taking an example from the field of economics, we see that strong economies have stable exchange rates but forcing an exchange rate to be stable will not necessarily produce a strong economy. Or, taking another example, this time from the field of management science, we can see that successful companies nearly always have good systems for assuring quality, but implementing a good quality system will not necessarily significantly improve your company.

Don't be afraid of emphasizing an aspect of the team culture in an extreme way, if that aspect of the culture reinforces a principle you feel very strongly about. However, be highly selective of any aspect you choose to highlight in an extreme fashion. I know of very few cultures that have *numerous,* extreme aspects.

A reinforcing culture

It is a good idea to align the team's culture with your leadership principles, and to use it to reinforce other key aspects of your management approach. In managing such business aspects as customer service or the financial bottom line, you will probably have to adopt a technique described in management-speak as *loose/tight.* That is, you probably should choose a few key factors to control tightly and leave all other factors under much looser control. For example, consider the financial controls within your organization—I will bet that you can instantly identify where tight financial controls exist, be they in the area of capital expenditure, cash flow, margins, volume, or some combination of them. Now think about which of the controls you exercise within your team are naturally suited to cultural reinforcement. One area might be peer review, as was the case on a team I managed. I needed to improve the quality of reports produced by my team and made peer review a principle that came to permeate the culture. After a period of time, it would have been unthinkable for someone to send a report out without having it reviewed first by an informal panel of peers.

A change-oriented culture

It will come as no surprise to the reader to be told that change is an ever-present feature of most successful companies. One of the greatest challenges that a manager faces is in pushing through necessary change within his or her team. So how do you, as a front-line manager, create a change-oriented culture? The following suggestions should help:

- Communicate your vision of the future direction so that it truly becomes the vision of the team. (Change should be seen as the necessary price of achieving the vision.)
- Embrace the change yourself, demonstrating through your actions that change is inevitable.
- Confront those who actively oppose change. (I use the word *confront* to mean that you, as manager, must not ignore people who resist change but not to mean that you should be confrontational. Explain why the change must happen and make it clear that, while the principle of the change is nonnegotiable, you are happy to discuss the tactics for implementing the change.)
- Develop a culture that *genuinely* tolerates honorable failure. (Management gurus constantly stress this point that honorable failure must be tolerated, and most organizations pay lip service to this idea, but their actions usually betray the shallowness of their under-standing of the concept of tolerating failure. Within the narrow confines of your team, you must ensure that those who fail honorably are not penalized, but, if appropriate, are rewarded with increased pay, a promo-tion, or other tangible aspects of their careers.)
- Lastly, help the team to realize that many of the reasons given for not changing exist only in team members' heads. (It is all too easy for you and the team to convince yourselves that change is not possible. "We will never get approval for this" can easily be used as the excuse to keep the status quo. In reality, your organization will sel-dom stop you from pursuing your vision, but you and the team will have to accept the risk of failure. Asking permission is usually asking someone else to accept the risk of failure, so no wonder the answer is usually no.)

*Develop a culture that genuinely tolerates
honorable failure.*

An elite culture

Many strong cultures think of themselves as an elite group.
This attitude can be valuable as it means that the culture sets
very high standards for itself, which can lead to high-quality
output. There is, however, a less positive side. Elite groups
tend to be very insular and often regard those outside their culture as "useless" or "stupid." Outsiders typically view someone in an elite group as "arrogant" and "overbearing." By
ensuring that your personal behavior is always tolerant and
respectful of people outside the culture, and by going out of
your way to show you disapprove of intolerance of outsiders,
you can go a long way to counteracting this natural tendency.

A respectful culture

Strong cultures can be very intolerant of those who do not conform to their behavioral norms. A typical example would be
the hard-driving culture that expects people to work long
hours and weekends, and to take work home. Another exam-

143

ple might be a culture in which team members aggressively challenge each other's views. Personally, I dislike this intolerant aspect in many strong cultures I have encountered, but I have to say that those cultures have usually flourished in spite of their intolerance. By standing up for individuality, a frontline manager can do a lot to imbue tolerance of individuality and diversity into the team culture.

Imbue tolerance of individuality and
diversity into the team culture.

HOW TO CREATE OR CHANGE A CULTURE

An implication of the Golden Rule of Management is that what you, as manager, spend your time doing will send a very strong message to the team about your priorities. A common mistake I see time and again is that managers involve *themselves* in the pursuit of new business opportunities. There is nothing fundamentally wrong in this, but if your involvement gets to the stage that you spend little or no time taking an interest in your team's existing core business and its customers, then you can expect those working for your existing customers to feel thoroughly unappreciated. In the rest of this section, I discuss the tools and techniques you can use to create the culture you want.

Management processes

One of the most important tools you have at your disposal is the detailed design of the procedures and processes within your team. Changing processes can have a major impact on the culture. For example, you may wish to change the team's attitude toward customer service. Consider the impact of allowing staff members who interact directly with customers to have delegated authority to resolve some customer complaints "on the spot" without reference to you or anyone else in authority. Do you trust your staff with such authority? Just how much authority are you willing to delegate? Do you think you need additional processes to manage the risk that the delegated authority will be mistakenly applied? Is your staff sufficiently aware of the big picture to exercise such authority properly? Are staff members sufficiently well trained to exercise such authority safely?

Addressing these issues will lead to team members growing increasingly aware of the level to which they personally are responsible for customer satisfaction, and staff responsibility will quickly become ingrained as part of the cultural approach to customer service. Although this example is a simple one, it illustrates the key role that processes can play in defining the team culture.

Pay and promotion

Like it or not, your implementation of staff pay increases and promotions will seriously impact the culture of your team. Pay increases and promotions will be viewed as a strong sign of the sorts of behavior that you value highly enough to reward.

Recruitment

An area in which I encourage you to invest your own time is recruitment. The kind of staff member you try to recruit sends a very strong message to the rest of the team. Your personal involvement will show that you take a genuine interest in the future of the team. Your involvement in recruitment is also the key to the level of diversity you want the culture to embrace. A common failing of strong leaders is to recruit clones of themselves, which reinforces the fact that the culture will tend to be a reflection of a specific leader's failings as well as strengths. Consider your current staff in order to identify which members are best suited to starting a project, which are good at working on a mature project, and which are skilled at putting the finishing touches on projects. Although not a rule cast in stone, it is generally true that the rare breed of people who can finish projects have quiet, undemonstrative personalities, whereas project starters frequently have a more flashy style. It is your job to ensure that you get an appropriately broad mix of staff into the team.

It is also your job to ensure that you do not allow any feelings of insecurity about your own qualifications to discourage the recruitment of outstanding, highly skilled staff: Do *not* view such staff as a threat. It has been my observation that good people recruit better people, but people who are not confident of their own skills recruit people who are less capable than themselves.

Recruitment is an interesting example of how cultures can become self-perpetuating. A strongly defined culture will be attractive to like-minded recruits and will tend to repel those who would not fit in. If someone is recruited who does not fit in, then a strong culture tends to expel him or her. Although the expulsion may not be physical, someone who does not fit in probably will not thrive on the team, and will often leave of his or her own accord.

Staff retention

Retaining the staff you recruit, especially the best staff, is obviously as important as recruiting them in the first place, but many managers underestimate the financial cost of high staff turnover. A strong culture can have a dramatic and positive effect on staff retention. Although industrial psychologists have long recognized that workers are motivated by the tangible aspects of their environment that enhance their working lives, workers are also motivated by the need to feel a sense of belonging. This may sound a bit spiritual, but a sense of belonging is a powerful force that can generate great staff loyalty. Anyone who has earned a position of respect within a strong culture will think long and hard before giving that up to move to a new job, where he or she will have to rebuild such a position from scratch.

Physical surroundings

Managers often underestimate what effect physical surroundings have on productivity. Although you, as a front-line manager, will often be severely constrained by your organization's policies on work space and accommodations, it is likely you can find significant wiggle room to adapt the surroundings to better suit the culture you want. A reorganization of an open-plan office area to get rid of individual cubicles and create groups of desks, the allocation of an informal meeting area for coffee breaks, the addition of whiteboards, or the allocation of rooms for impromptu meetings can all improve the environment in which your people work. One reason that office accommodation raises such passions is that workers understand how important it is to their efficiency and happiness. It is a pity that more managers and organizations do not understand this as passionately.

If the area your team occupies is divided into physically separate units—that is, different floors, separate buildings, or even separate sites—you most likely will find that the separate units will form separate sub-cultures. A natural outcome, this really is not something to be afraid of—do not react by trying to enforce a totally homogeneous culture.

Your personal accommodation also sends a very strong message to the team. If team members all work in an open plan and you have a luxurious private office, what do you think they will read into this? Sure, you may need a private space to conduct confidential conversations and telephone calls, but sharing the open-plan accommodation and dedicating a small meeting room for private meetings and conversations sends a much more positive message than disparate accommodations ever can communicate.

There is a possibly apocryphal story about a new chief executive at Hewlett-Packard whose first action was to remove the door from his private office and leave it propped up against the wall. The number of times I have heard this story bears testament to the significance that physical surroundings have on a culture. The story also provides a good example of how management myths and legends are a powerful way in which cultures become self-sustaining. As new members of the culture hear such anecdotes, they receive a powerful message about the underlying principles of the culture.

Managers often underestimate what effect
physical surroundings have on productivity.

Social events

A rich source of myths and legends, sometimes of the embarrassing kind, are team social events. The social dimension is one that must be adapted to the individual circumstances of any particular team. Here are some suggestions that might be worth considering:

- If you, as manager, receive a bonus that is based on the performance of the team as well as on your own performance, invest part of that bonus in sponsoring several team social events. You could organize these to include yourself or offer to buy drinks and food for a party the team members organize for themselves.
- Encourage casual events that require little organizing, such as an evening out bowling or at a restaurant, or, if you are a Brit like me, a trip to the pub.
- Sponsor casual events that require a little more organizing, like a ball game or backyard barbecue.

The activities listed above will probably involve team members and their partners. The next batch of ideas can involve just team members.

- Take people out for a meal or drinks if they have been working late.
- Invite random groups of people out for lunch, but be careful that you do not include the same people each time.
- Arrange a lunchtime buffet, either for purely social reasons or to hold an informal team meeting as people eat.

THE DANGERS OF A STRONG CULTURE

In all of the above, I have intended to convey the idea that strong cultures are a good thing. In general, I do believe this. Strong cultures have many desirable features but they also have some potentially undesirable aspects, as addressed in the remainder of this section.

Rejection of individualism

Strong cultures can exert enormous peer pressure on group members, forcing them to reject their individual preferences in order to conform with the ways of the group. Two damaging examples that I have personally seen follow:

- A culture where everyone works long hours can be threatening to someone who either cannot or does not want to work such long hours.
- A culture that has strong social or sports elements can be threatening to people who do not want to participate.

A culture that has strong social or sports elements can be threatening to people who do not want to participate.

Institutionalization of weaknesses

Ideally, team members should cover for each other's weaknesses. When a culture reinforces a particular sort of behavior, then any weaknesses associated with that behavior tend not to be managed well. In a culture that is very competitive, for example, it is unlikely that anyone will suggest a compromise solution as an alternative to a fight to the end.

Group-think

People functioning in a strong culture will sometimes think and act as one. This can be very positive, but when the group behaves in a negative fashion, exhibiting anti-management attitudes or paranoia, for example, then group-think can be very dangerous.

TWO PLEAS

Before closing this chapter, I have an unusual request: a plea for intolerance. I ask each and every one of you to be extremely intolerant of anyone who breaks with the fundamental principles of the culture you establish. For example, if integrity is a cornerstone of the culture, then those who play fast and loose with integrity should be nailed to the wall as an example to others.

I also must submit a plea for high standards and ask that you avoid the temptation to turn a blind eye to minor transgressions, such as bending the rules on expenses, minor health and safety infractions, and jokes made in bad taste. One of the reasons that you cannot be "one of the gang" is that, as leader of the culture, you must set high standards, both in your own behavior and in your reactions to team members bending the rules.

SUMMARY

The principle that underlies the culture of your team is

Consistent behavior by the leader sets the tone for the culture.

Your consistent behavior will tell the team what you approve of and what you condemn, but do reinforce expected behavior with words. Whether you like it or not, you may find that your team takes on some of your personality traits.

You should make a conscious decision about the sort of culture that you want to create. Two areas to be paid particular attention are the team's approach to customer care and the team's attitude toward change.

In changing a team's culture, one of the most effective techniques is to change the processes within the team.

Be aware that even subtle signals will have an impact on your team's culture. Issues such as whether you have a private office and how you allocate your time will affect the culture of your team.

Suggested Reading

Collins, James C., and Jerry I. Porras. *Built to Last: Successful Habits of Visionary Companies.* New York: HarperBusiness, 1994.

> A well-researched book that examines what distinguishes the very best companies from other good companies. Although the subject matter is about large organizations, many of the lessons apply to small teams as well.

DeMarco, Tom, and Timothy Lister. *Peopleware: Productive Projects and Teams,* 2nd ed. New York: Dorset House Publishing, 1999.

> A provocative study of productivity in the software industry, *Peopleware* has the best and, to my mind, most amusing discussion of the effects of office space on productivity that I have read.

Peters, Thomas J., and Robert H. Waterman, Jr. *In Search of Excellence: Lessons from America's Best-Run Companies.* New York: Harper & Row, 1982.

> Similar in scope to *Built to Last.* Published in 1982, the examples in this famous management book are now dated, but the underlying analysis of company cultures is still relevant.

CHAPTER 8

Managing a
Failing Team

Every profession has its exciting and glamorous jobs. For front-line managers, being brought in to turn around a failing team has to be one of the most stimulating jobs there is.

Called turnaround management, the act of turning around a failing team is exciting and glamorous, in part at least, because of its uniqueness:

Every failing team represents a unique set of problems, and hence a unique challenge to the manager.

The challenge of a turnaround is exhilarating; the uniqueness makes it all the more memorable. There are, however, certain aspects of turning around a team that are not unique, aspects that in fact tend to recur frequently. By knowing a range of useful techniques that can be applied as appropriate to the individual circumstances you will encounter, and by understanding how turnaround management differs from other forms of management, you, as a front-line manager, can help assure that the experience will be exciting, glamorous, *and successful.*

TURNAROUND–MANAGEMENT CHARACTERISTICS

Turning around a team usually presents some particularly challenging problems to you as the new manager. The following scenario is by no means unlikely:

- The team is in a highly dysfunctional state with a breakdown in communication within the team, and a breakdown in trust between the team and higher management.
- The team's products are not financially viable.
- Upper management either has lost patience with the team's performance or is rapidly losing patience, putting you under pressure to deliver results fast.

This sort of situation means that you have to face problems of much greater magnitude than a new team leader normally faces and, to make matters worse, usually also means that you will be under greater pressure to deliver results fast. Despite your newness to your position, you will need to make hard and fast decisions, ones that are likely to cause considerable pain to the team. In order to get the job done successfully and within tight time constraints, you may have to *impose* your will on the team. Frequently traumatic and usually unsettling, imposing one's will rarely seems intuitive. In fact, it is so difficult to do that you may wish to consider using some or all of the techniques described in the following eight steps when you find yourself in the situation of having to impose your will on the team.

EIGHT NOT-SO-SIMPLE STEPS

Strange as the comparison may strike some readers, I maintain that the following eight-step recovery plan can be as much a career-saver for struggling turnaround managers as ten-step recovery plans are lifesavers for gamblers, alcoholics, and other addicts:

1. *Understand your terms of reference.* Decode management's perception of the team's problems and its expec-

tations for improvement. How much time do you have? How will your success or failure be measured?

2. *Gather the data that will allow you to understand the team's problems.* You need to understand individual team members, the team culture, the financial status of the team's business, the customers' perceptions of the team, and the perceptions of other groups in the organization.

3. *Institute emergency actions.* You often cannot wait until you have a full understanding of all the team's problems before implementing a recovery plan. Take action to stop the situation from deteriorating further, and start rebuilding morale and a positive momentum.

4. *Identify the team's key problems.* Failing teams tend to have an abundance of problems, not one single problem. Once you find a major problem, keep looking; there are often multiple major problems that need to be solved.

5. *Decide if the team can, and should, be saved.* This step is an especially hard one. Having been sent in to turn a failing team around, you will naturally feel that you can only be a success if you save the team. Frequently, however, you will find that the team's business situation has changed radically—for example, the reason the team was created may no longer exist, or so many key staff members have left, that it is better to cut the organization's losses and disband the team. It may be your duty to close down the team in an orderly fashion if that is the best decision from your organization's point of view.

6. *Create a credible strategy and vision that will save the team.* You must find a viable set of products and services that can sustain the team's business, and you must be able to solve those problems that are destroying the team's ability to successfully deliver those products and services.

7. *Implement the strategy and vision.* Having found solutions to the team's problems, you must create a plan of action to quickly get from the current situation to a viable future.

155

8. *Leave.* Once it is clear that the team is likely to survive, it is probable that you are not the best person to lead it into its future. The styles of turnaround artists are so very different from the styles of long-term leaders that it is often impossible for the same person to make the transition from the turnaround leader who imposes his or her will on the team, to the long-term leader who commands by virtue of the respect of the team's members.

Step 1: Understand your terms of reference.

It is essential that you understand your own upper-level management's perception of what problems you must solve. You should not assume that your manager's perception is necessarily correct, and hence you should keep an open mind as you start to gather data about the team, and begin to identify the nature of the problems it faces. At the end of the day, however, it is your managers you will have to convince, so know what preconceptions they hold.

In addition to understanding your terms of reference, clarify the parameters under which you are working. By answering questions such as the following, you can identify key parameters:

- What is the minimum improvement your management would regard as a success?
- How much time do you have to turn the team around?
- What authority do you have? Do you have the authority to remove team members, for example?

Usually, it is best to clarify these parameters, but there may be circumstances in which you can benefit from a lack of clarity. Decide on a case-by-case basis whether clarity works for or against you. If you decide that it is best to understand your terms of reference clearly, then it is likely to benefit you to negotiate a sensible approach to your management's expectations of how fast you can effect an improvement.

In general, you will want to negotiate as much time as possible. A useful technique is to negotiate a deadline for completion of some preliminary phase, with the deadline expressed in a form such as: "In two months, I will meet with you to discuss my analysis of the team's problems. I will make a recommendation of whether I think that the team can be saved and, if I think it can be saved, I will present a draft strategy for turning the team around." At such a meeting, you can then explore the metrics by which the team's improvement will be measured.

Step 2: Gather the data that will allow you to understand the team's problems.

Gathering information requires that you consider two key issues: What information do you need to discover? and, Where will you find this information?

Identify what information you need to discover. Ask, What key problems does the team face that you need to solve if the team is to become a success in the eyes of your management and customers? To get the information you need, you will want to distinguish between causes and effects. Using a medical analogy, this means you will need to distinguish between symptoms, such as a headache, and the root cause, stress, for example. This is not to say that you should not treat symptoms—there is nothing wrong with taking aspirin to stop the headache as long as you also treat the underlying cause.

Notice that I included a qualifier above: "in the eyes of your management and customers." Step 2 introduces my first mention of customers in this chapter and the qualifier makes an intentional and very significant point: Because a dysfunctional team will frequently focus on internal problems, an important technique in turning the team around is to get the team to refocus on what value it delivers to its customers. A very good starting point is to know what your customers think are the problems with the team's deliverables.

Identify what people inside and outside the team think are the problems, and what they think should be done to solve them. This two-directional question relates to a previous point in which I noted that you need to find out what the real problems are. Find out what your stakeholders think the problems are. Ask the stakeholders what they think you should do about the problems. They have probably been thinking about these problems for a lot longer than you have, so the answer may be there for the asking. In reality, it is unlikely that you will have the answer served up to you on a plate, but many of the key ingredients to a solution may well emerge from talking to your stakeholders.

Identify which staff members are key to your team's business. Even if it has not been explicitly announced that you have been brought in to turn the team around, you will have to get team members to accept that there are significant problems to address, which will probably involve painful changes. A bit like recovering from a gambling addiction or alcoholism, the first step to recovery is to acknowledge that you have a problem. Major change is very unsettling to staff and there is a danger that people will start looking for other jobs. To minimize the danger, tell key staff members that their job is safe (if that is the case), and let them know that they are key to the business. Remember that key staff members are not just the flamboyant superstars, but also the less flashy back-room types who keep the business running.

Identify which staff members are key "opinion-formers" in the team. Every team has a few members whose views have a great impact on the culture of the team. Once you have a vision and strategy for saving the team, you will find that if you can sell your strategy to these opinion-formers, then you are more than halfway to selling it to the whole team.

Assess the financial state of the team's business. Although this book focuses on the people aspects of management, I hope I have been clear throughout that a front-line manager must never lose sight of his or her responsibility to run the business aspects of the team properly. Among the many important people issues associated with turning a failing team around, perhaps the single most important matter is to ensure that you, as manager, have a credible business strategy for the future. Start by looking at the current financial status of the business, examining financial statements and looking over the books—if they exist. Chances are, if the team is failing, its members probably have no clear idea of its true financial status. As manager, you need to find out the missing details—fast.

Find out the team's history. There are two reasons why knowing as much as possible about the team's history makes good sense. First, it is often easier to spot the reasons for current problems if you understand the events that led up to them. Second, it is almost always easier to get team members to open up to you if they know you understand what has led to the current difficulties. Members of dysfunctional teams often have problems communicating with each other and with people outside the team. This breakdown in communications may be part of the cause of the team's problems, or it may be an effect of those problems. In addition, a dysfunctional team may have a lot of pent-up hostility. Trust between team members and their management may have broken down completely and, at least to begin with, you will be viewed by the team as one of "them," not one of "us." Finding out the history helps you to show your commitment to the team and is a good way to solicit your staff's views on what has gone wrong and what has gone right.

A dysfunctional team may have a lot of pent-up hostility.

Identify whom you should ask for historical detail. There are many sources from whom to solicit information.

The outgoing manager: It is surprising how often turn-around managers overlook asking their predecessor for information. I think the oversight is largely an issue of embarrassment: Turnaround managers frequently worry that the previous leader will see himself or herself as a failure and will resent being questioned by the new managers, believing that they have been brought in to sort out the mess he or she created. My experience is that outgoing managers are often willing to offer generous assistance, and will be flattered that their opinion is valued.

Team members: As I outlined above in the discussion of dysfunctional teams, conversations with team members may be difficult, but if you behave in a straightforward and honest way, many will respond openly and eagerly. You will do yourself and your staff a disservice if you shy away from such difficult questions as

- What do you think has gone wrong?
- What do we do best for our customers? What do we do badly?
- What are the strengths and weaknesses of our products and services?
- Whose opinions in the team do you particularly respect?
- Whose professional judgment do you respect?
- If you were me, what would you do first?
- What is the biggest problem you face in doing your job as well as you would like?
- What annoys you most?
- Do you think you are doing the right job?
- What do you think we should do to make things work better?

Notice that all these sample questions are so-called open questions, which cannot be answered by a simple yes or no, but which will tend to make individual staff members express their opinions.

Do not omit anyone from this dialogue. Often, junior staff, support staff, and younger staff members will offer a fresher view and a different perspective from the more experienced staff.

Non-team members employed within your organization: This group of non-team members can include your managers, your peers, and support staff such as Finance, Personnel, and Human Resources. Ask questions similar to those you ask team members but you can be more blunt with these non-team members:

- Who do you think are my key players?
- Who do you think are weak performers?
- Who do you think I can and cannot trust?
- Who may try to undermine me?

In addition, you will need to seek specific information, such as financial data from the Finance department.

Your customers: Customers may prove to be your greatest source of insight into your business problems, but gathering data by asking them questions takes tact and strategy. You will have to decide how open you can be with customers about the fact that your organization recognizes there are serious problems that need to be sorted.

Failing teams tend to throw up masses of urgent problems, which the team will look to you to fire-fight. As a result, time for gathering data can get squeezed out of your agenda. You must be disciplined enough to keep sufficient time in your daily schedule for this inevitably time-consuming data-gathering exercise.

Step 3: Institute emergency actions.

Although every turnaround situation has characteristics that are unique to it, there are some issues that come up time and again, requiring the front-line manager to take swift and decisive action. The most drastic action necessitates cutting staff, costs, or both.

Assess, and if necessary cut, your cost base. It is very likely that a failing team has problems that affect its bottom line. It is a sad fact that the fastest way to improve the bottom line usually is to cut costs. If you decide you need to implement a cost-cutting program, the following advice may help you plan what actions to take and how to present the decision you reached:

- Avoid cuts that directly affect your customers.
- Communicate to your team your rationale for why the cuts are needed.
- Try to ensure that the cuts will be viewed as fair.
- Follow your organization's guidelines for staff transfer or termination—do not be tempted to cut corners! ·
- If you must remove staff, pick people who are not likely to be key to your future strategy.
- Show that you are personally sharing in any painful cost-cutting measures—for example, don't fly business class.
- Try to get all the pain out of the way in one pass—coming back later for a second round of cuts can be devastating to team morale, which in fact may improve if people see the cuts as the start of the turnaround.

Pick low-hanging fruit to increase revenues. Although it is generally easier to cut costs than to increase revenues, look for ways to squeeze additional income out of the team's current output or products. Look for low-hanging fruit in the form of existing business that can be developed without a significant investment of the team's time or resources. You may be surprised at what you find.

In fact, even in successful, financially healthy teams, relatively simple methods of increasing revenue get overlooked; it is even more likely that such opportunities are being missed in a failing team. Ask yourself and your staff questions such as, Can we sell additional products and services to existing customers? Can we update an existing product or service? Can we adapt an existing product or service to a new market? With your team, actively search for such opportunities and pursue them vigorously.

Start turning members of your team into winners. A saying I particularly like is, "Team spirit is an illusion created by success." But as much as I like the message, it doesn't capture the whole truth. In my experience, the best way to create a winning team is to start winning. If you can set a worthwhile, challenging objective and then achieve it, you will probably see a dramatic improvement in morale and team spirit. The objective you choose should focus on delivering value to a customer, because this will start the team focusing outward and will help stop unhealthy, introspective attitudes and behavior.

Reestablish lost momentum. Most failing teams tend to drift, and team members will see little progress; often, they will perceive that the situation is deteriorating. It is very important to reestablish a sense of momentum at the earliest opportunity. Choose a few problems, even if they are relatively minor, and sort them out, looking especially at areas where progress can be made. You must personally ensure that quick progress is made on these issues.

Where possible, clear the decks and wipe the slate clean. A team that is in trouble generally has one or more long-term problems that are poisoning the morale of the team. It could be that a project deliverable is overdue, that there are two factions with a fundamental disagreement, that there is a personality clash between staff members, or that one part of the team blames another part for failing to deliver on a project. Whenever possible, identify the problem or problems, discuss solutions, and then get the team to move on, focusing on the future rather than constantly rehashing the past. If one problem is a missed deadline, for example, set a realistic replacement and direct the team to work toward meeting it.

Confront negativity and "teamicidal" behavior. As noted at the beginning of this chapter, turnaround management involves numerous situations in which a front-line manager will need to impose his or her will on the team. One time that this is particularly likely occurs when individuals on the team—or the team as a whole—feel as if they are losers and express negative feelings, or simply show little desire to get on with their work.

Turning around a team is never just a business exercise, and when a manager must address people-oriented issues as well as business issues, the job becomes all the more challenging. The team must know that you, as its manager, are confident that you can achieve your objectives. To do this, you may have to confront negativity, treading a narrow line between accepting and soliciting constructive criticism and rejecting destructive comments. How to determine when a comment is purely destructive can be difficult, but one measure is to assess the attitude in which the comments are made: Any comment that has the flavor of whining, moaning, blaming, defeatism, or the like, should be stamped on hard. My personal position is not as extreme as insisting that everyone sound positive, but I do believe the maxim that "if you cannot say something positive, then keep your mouth shut." If people continue to be vocally negative after you have expressed your views, then you should consider hard actions such as discipline, transfer, or dismissal.

Failing teams that develop behavioral patterns that severely undermine a positive team culture are said to be "teamicidal." For example, when one member of your team persistently bullies other members, you face a classic case of teamicidal behavior. I again recommend that you come down like the proverbial ton of bricks on any occurrences of teamicidal behavior.

Impose your will. Much of the behavior I have recommended above will set the right environment for you to exercise a high level of control over the team. To complete the turnaround, you need to back this up with other techniques, as described below:

- First, you need to adopt an appropriately decisive manner, showing the team that decisions are made speedily, but not hastily. Make a reasonable effort to ensure that decisions are based on accurate information that is as complete as time allows. Under no circumstances should you shift responsibility for decisions onto anyone else—*you* make the decisions and *you* take full responsibility for them. Stick to your decisions unless it becomes clear the decision needs changing, in which case, quickly change the decision without any outward sign of embarrassment at having gotten the original decision wrong. Try to adopt an attitude that says, "We are going to make mistakes—let's get on with it."

Adopt an appropriately decisive manner.

• Second, keep team members informed of what you are doing and why. Ensure that people know that you are not informing them in order to seek their approval, but rather to ensure that they can act appropriately because they know what is going on.

Step 4: Identify the team's key problems.

In order to identify your team's key difficulties, you will need to distinguish the issues that arise from a flawed business strategy from those caused by the poor implementation of a basically sound business proposition. If the business strategy is basically sound, you should be able to identify which are the key implementation issues that must be addressed in order to turn the team around. Assessing your team's implementation problems is not impossible. It is my belief that there are only a few implementation problems that may prove insoluble, the most common of which is the loss of key staff—a topic more fully discussed in Chapter 13, "Managing in the Real World."

Assessing the soundness of your team's business proposition is much harder. Although managers face so many business issues in the course of a project that it would take an entire book even to list them, there are certain basic items to consider. Here is a list of questions to ask team members:

- What products and services are now sold, and what could be sold in the future?
- Who are your existing customers?
- How would you classify your target customers?
- Who are your competitors and how do they compete with you?
- How do your customers perceive your products and services, and is that the perception you want?
- How do your customers differentiate your products and services from those of your competitors?
- How do you create the right perceptions in potential customers' minds?
- How do you price your services?
- How do your customers find out about your product and service offerings?

It is also important to track how the basics of the business proposition have changed over time. A business proposition that may have been valid some years ago may no longer be viable.

Step 5: Decide if the team can, and should, be saved.

There are, in my view, two likely and defendable scenarios for deciding that a team should be disbanded:

1. The staff capability that underpins the business of the team has fallen well below critical mass, and the cost and risk of trying to recreate that capability are too great given the likely benefits to your organization.
2. The business proposition underpinning the team is not viable, and the cost and risk of developing a viable business model are too great given the potential benefits of creating a new business model.

I once had the job of performing an investment appraisal for a British government project. While doing research for the task, I came across a comprehensive manual that described a rigorous process for analyzing a potential investment. The manual was a very sensible document that described how to do a fiendishly difficult job. One of the most valuable instructions in the manual advised that all investments be base-lined against what was called the *Do Nothing* option—that is, the option to make no investment whatsoever.

I believe that the Do Nothing option is as applicable in the context of turnaround management as it is in the field of investment, and suggest that you view the act of turning around a team as an investment decision by your organization. In Do Nothing terms, the baseline would be to disband the team. This means that you need to realistically estimate the costs and benefits of breaking up the team, and compare your proposed recovery plans against that baseline.

Step 6: Create a credible strategy and vision that will save the team.

Assuming that the team should be saved, your next step should be to create a strategy for its future. When analyzing how to move forward from the current position, you will have to assess and balance three different aspects:

1. You will need to consider how to solve whatever implementation problems the team faces, such as improving

margins, restoring momentum, improving morale, energizing the staff, improving customer service, winning more customers, recruiting key staff, and so on.

2. You will need to consider how to redesign the business proposition that underpins the team.
3. You will need to consider how to maintain or grow capability within the team.

Although all three aspects may challenge a new manager, the first two involve fairly standard business and people-oriented tasks—ones that should be familiar to readers. However, the third point might need looking at in a bit more detail: Capability can be defined as the sum of the expertise, experience, physical facilities, supporting infrastructure (work processes, for example), customers (past and present), and network of contacts that the team possesses.

What is the value of a capability? The value lies in the business opportunities that arise from that capability. It is relatively easy to decide to keep the team together if you can see the set of opportunities that will be developed within the recovery plan. What is more difficult is if you feel that the capability is valuable, but you cannot immediately see enough opportunities to create a viable recovery plan. In such circumstances, it may well be worth discussing with your management whether the organization wishes to maintain the capability for a period of time in the expectation that business opportunities will emerge in the future.

Step 7: Implement the strategy and vision.

How does implementing turnaround strategy and vision differ from "normal" management of a team? There are several distinguishing tasks that characterize this stage.

Handle time pressures. It is likely that you will have a greater amount of change to implement in a shorter period of time than normal. You do have the advantage that, in a turnaround situation, many staff members will accept your pushing through change in a very direct way, confirming that turnaround situations are typified by your having to impose your will on the team.

Adopt a "Management by Objectives" approach. I have deliberately hijacked this management-speak phrase because, in the turnaround situation, you need to remain very focused on the metrics that you have set to measure the success, or failure, of your recovery plan. Again, you have the advantage that most staff members will accept that meeting the team's targets is essential to the recovery of a failing team. You must ensure both that the whole team's targets and that individual members' targets are clear, precise, achievable, and measurable.

Maintain momentum and drive. In describing Step 3, above, I pointed out that it is relatively easy to stress urgency and hence maintain a high level of motivation in the team. At this somewhat later stage, you will need to convince the team that you expect all members to stay in overdrive for an extended period of time. If you push your team hard, you must make it evident that you are willing to push yourself hardest of all. At this point in the turnaround effort, some preferred practices may need to be thrown out the window: You are likely to need to work very long hours yourself and you may well need to ask your team members to work very long hours as well. You may also need to personally take an interest in the details of the operations of the team. In this case, micromanagement may be required as you may need to constantly check and recheck that deadlines will be met.

Maintain an outward focus. Be alert for any recurrence of inward-looking factionalism, bullying, and blame, and jump from an enormous height on the first signs of any such behavior. Because the team needs to be focused on delivering results to customers and meeting your business targets, you must demonstrate that you are looking for results, not excuses. Consequently, you may need to say, "Don't just bring me the problem, bring me your proposed solution." Not only do you need to ensure that people own up to problems, you also must make them think about their responsibility to solve those problems as well.

Focus, focus, and focus. One of the truisms of management still applies: You can only achieve a few things at any one time. This reality means that you must very carefully choose the things you wish to achieve. Because you will have to resolve problems very quickly, you will need to sequence your priorities carefully, stating your goals so that everyone can hear you: "I will do this; and then I can do that; and then . . ." By emphasizing focus, focus, focus, you will have mandated an approach far superior to starting everything together and then losing focus.

Avoid bad managerial behavior. Admittedly, the directive to avoid bad managerial behavior is made somewhat tongue-in-cheek to make the point that, when turning around a team, the price you pay for ignoring many of the normal techniques of good management is greatly magnified. This risk—along with the fact that there is little margin for error—is one of the reasons that turning around a team is so exciting.

Although you undoubtedly can come up with a long list of examples of behavior that managers should never allow themselves to exhibit, my short list of actions that are certain to have a very detrimental effect includes the following:

- dishonesty
- lack of clarity
- lack of feedback to staff members
- indecisiveness
- blaming staff

Manage your managers' expectations. Early in this chapter, I stressed how important it is for the front-line manager to find out what his or her own management perceives the team's problems to be. It is equally important to keep your managers informed about the turnaround process. Your managers have the power of life and death over your team, and it would be highly irresponsible, almost to the point of being criminal, if you succeed in turning the team around, to then have your management pull the rug out from under your feet. Please do not think that this is an unlikely scenario: The team is no longer a failing team if, and only if, your management says so. Keeping your management informed means you need to market and sell the turnaround to your management. The problem is, you are likely to be so busy that you may forget to do this, but don't forget! To do so would be a big mistake.

Step 8: Leave.

Once the team has turned around, can you as manager adapt from managing by means of a well-nigh dictatorial style, to the more usual long-term style of managing by virtue of having the respect of your team? Before you decide whether you can change your style, think about your answer to the following personal question:

Do you really want to stay with the team after the turnaround? Turning around a team will undoubtedly give you a great buzz. Do you want to return to the mundane world of day-to-day management? There are managers who become adrenaline junkies who should move on from one such challenge to the next. Even if you do not want to become a full-time "turnaround artist," you may find it easier to return to normal management in another team rather than to stay with the team you have just resuscitated. One reason for this is the fear that you and the team will keep harking back to the golden days of the turnaround.

Can you change your style? If you decide you want to stay with the team, you will need to change your style gradually from the dictatorial to a more consensual approach. Some managers can adapt their style to the requirements of a particular situation, but there are others who do one style really well, but cannot adapt. I am strongly of the opinion that the dictatorial style is not appropriate for long-term leadership, and if that is your only game, it probably would be best for you to implement Step 8 and leave.

Do you have a choice? It may be that your organization put you in position only to turn the team around and that your management expects to move you elsewhere afterwards. If you were brought in from outside the organization, your management's view may even be as extreme as expecting you to leave the organization. In the best of worlds, you will have negotiated this eventuality at the time you were hired. In other cases, you will need to assess all your options, and select the best one.

SUMMARY

Turnaround management assumes a situation in which you will need to impose your will on the team.

Adopt an eight-step plan to turn around a failing team:

1. Understand your terms of reference.
2. Gather the data that will allow you to understand the team's problems.
3. Institute emergency actions.
4. Identify the team's key problems.
5. Decide if the team can, and should, be saved.
6. Create a credible strategy and vision that will save the team.
7. Implement the strategy and vision.
8. Leave.

Although there are many important people issues, the single most important aspect of turning around a team is to correctly analyze the business problems and create a credible strategy for the future.

You will need to identify your key staff members, so you can focus your efforts on keeping them. You also will need to identify the key opinion-formers in the team, because you will have to sell your vision of the future to them.

Two key tasks that must be undertaken in attempting to turn a team around are to first confront any negativity within the team, and then to maintain the momentum for change.

CHAPTER 9

Organizing Your Team (and Yourself)

Many management books concentrate on the mechanics of management. I tend to think of this as the "what" of management. In this book, I focus more on the principles that underpin good management, which I think of as the "why" of management, and use many of the "whats" to illustrate the "whys." This chapter, which begins with a look at how you can organize yourself, will mop up a few of the "whats" that do not appear elsewhere in the book.

ORGANIZING YOURSELF

Time management

I must confess that although I am someone who has taken "Managing Your Time" courses, I seem remarkably resistant to their techniques. Apart from writing lists of things to do, I use few of the well-known time-management techniques. If you are less resistant than I am to good time-management practices, then you should certainly take a course or read one of the many excellent books on the subject. These courses and books give sound advice on how to get the most out of your time, but be forewarned: *No matter how well you manage your time, it is unlikely that you can do everything you want to do.*

This universal truth means that in order to be effective as a front-line manager, you must employ techniques to actually reduce the amount of work that you personally do. Possible ways to reduce your own workload include

- delegating tasks and supervisory responsibilities
- reducing your level of perfectionism on appropriate tasks
- dropping low-priority tasks

Which tasks and supervisory responsibilities can be delegated depend on the specifics of your corporate culture and management, and on the capabilities of your staff members. There are no tips I can provide that would be more useful than what your own instincts and observations tell you about delegating. However, I can offer some help with the second and third points.

Reduce your level of perfectionism on appropriate tasks. I have seen a number of managers work themselves into the ground because they had no notion of doing a job merely *well enough*. Put bluntly, a lot of the work you will spend your time doing is not vitally important to the future of the team. You need to discipline yourself to identify work that can be done less well, and then ruthlessly limit the amount of time you put into such tasks.

Drop low-priority tasks. I once conducted an experiment in connection with the volume of daily e-mail I received from other parts of my organization demanding answers of various kinds. I ignored them all and waited to see how many people chased me. Approximately 90 percent never chased me. Of the remaining 10 percent, I replied with as brief a message as possible to about 80 percent and then dealt diligently with the remaining 20 percent I thought important. Result: I dealt with about 2 percent of the e-mail diligently.

For fear of incriminating myself irrevocably, I will not describe other experiments I conducted to determine what jobs I could ignore without getting into trouble. I am not recommending that you copy my somewhat irresponsible behavior; my reason for mentioning these experiments is to prompt you to think carefully about your priorities, and consider whether some of your lower priority jobs can be left undone so that you can give more time to the really important jobs.

As you attempt to identify which tasks cannot be dropped safely, be aware of which tasks your boss is particularly interested in. To be brutally cynical, I think it is always worth finding out which of your tasks could impact your boss's bonus, because you drop those at your peril!

Fire fighting

There will be times when you feel that the job of a manager is to constantly fight fires. No sooner do you sit down at your desk than team members descend on you with problems requiring a decision from you. It is important that you ensure that the constant calls on your attention to fire-fight urgent, day-to-day problems do not become so dominant that there is no time left to think about longer-term strategic issues. It may be that you will have to think about such important, long-term issues at home, or that you will need to move yourself and the people with whom you should discuss such issues away from the pressures of the office. Whatever technique you adopt, you must make time for addressing important, albeit non-urgent, jobs.

Record-keeping

Although the way a manager sets up his or her filing system is a matter of individual preference, I do want to mention one technique that has served me well during my career. I keep a personal logbook, a bound book with numbered pages in which I write the salient points of each day's activities. At the end of each day, I spend five-to-ten minutes noting any issues that could come back to bite me—for example, any discussion with an under-performing staff member or anyone suspected of misconduct. I cannot remember how many times my logbook has kept me out of trouble, but it's a lot. Being able to defend my record of events, backed by my logbook, has often stopped a complaint in its tracks.

Stress management

How you live your life can help you to cope with the stress that comes with a management job, but there can be some hidden dangers in a healthy life-style. While I certainly do not recommend that you give in to a desire to become a junk-food addict and couch potato or that you avoid proper diet and exercise, there's a lesson to be learned in the experience I had many years ago when I started to worry that I was not coping properly with an extended period of pressure. I enrolled in a stress-management course, and started eating properly, swimming daily, doing muscle-toning exercises, and practicing relaxation techniques. The program worked brilliantly and I felt I was coping much better with the pressure at work. So what did I do? I worked harder and longer, putting myself right back in the pressure cooker.

Practicing stress-management techniques can be like improving the suspension on your automobile and fitting it with wide tires. If you use the improved suspension and tires so that you can go around corners faster, when your vehicle eventually loses traction, you are going that much faster and the accident tends to be worse than it would have been if you had not modified your automobile. If you do use healthy-living techniques, use them to cope with the *same pressure better*, not to handle more and more pressure.

Lightweight Processes

In the universe of the front-line manager, there exist many different styles of management, two of which are diametrically opposed. For the first, the manager creates a set of processes to keep people from blundering, making mistakes, and otherwise screwing up. For the second, the manager accepts that mistakes are an inevitable part of life (especially if people must be pushed to the limits of their performance) and sets up lightweight processes that catch those mistakes and rectify them quickly. You have probably guessed from the way I have phrased the two styles that I am a believer in the second approach. The second way is made very much easier if you have created an agile team culture that is capable of reacting to mistakes quickly.

The key to establishing successful lightweight processes is to create an appropriate level of visibility. The most valuable technique I have found is to hold monthly progress meetings at which all projects are reviewed. I always insist on "exception reporting," by which I mean that all reports should be of the form "everything is okay except . . ." This process not only draws attention to difficult aspects, but it also gets the team used to thinking about potential problems on a regular basis.

Create an appropriate level of visibility.

ORGANIZING TEAM STRUCTURE

The structure of your team is best built around the skills of the staff you have. The approach of designing an idealized team structure, and then trying to fill all the posts within that structure, can only work if the team is large enough that you are likely to find enough staff with the requisite skills. Assuming that you are at the same level as front-line managers in most organizations and that you won't have much opportunity to fill posts with people of your own choosing, you probably will need to build a team structure around the people you have at hand.

Focus on the probability that you will have only a limited number of staff members who first can take on a particular role, task, or project, and then can be relied on to do the job well. You must face the fact that once you deploy these key staff members to high-priority areas, other roles, tasks, and projects may not run as smoothly as they would if a key staff member were involved.

Delegating Responsibilities

Two roles you may want to delegate are those of *operations manager* and *routine personnel manager.* Of these, the more important to delegate may be the operations management role because it can be both time-consuming and disproportionately stressful. In addition, the type of person who is a good leader frequently does not have the right personality to handle the day-to-day detailed operations of the team. If this characterization describes you, you would be wise to delegate operations management at one of a number of levels. At one extreme, you may be able to pass off most of the responsibilities to a professional business administrator. At the other extreme, you might retain the major responsibilities and assign a reliable office assistant to execute the bulk of the routine operations duties.

In discussing delegated operations roles, I do not intend to suggest that the delegated duties would necessarily occupy all of a person's time; they may well be part-time responsibilities.

Tasks that must be performed as part of routine personnel management similarly may only require delegation of someone part-time. It is an especially good idea to delegate such tasks if you are not particularly skilled at interpersonal relationships, but even if you do not feel the need to delegate many personnel management responsibilities, there is an advantage in having someone within your team who regularly talks to staff members about their concerns. If your organization has a good Personnel or Human Resources department, you may wish to allocate some personnel responsibilities to that department.

As the team's leader, you will often have to balance the needs of the individual against the good of the team. No matter how skilled you are at interpersonal relationships, you will be viewed as the boss because you *are* the boss—and the boss is the person who has all-important hiring and firing power. Staff members may find it less easy to be totally open with you than they would with an independent personnel representative. Consequently, someone who functions independent of you as personnel manager can advocate the needs of the individual, or can raise an issue of general concern without identifying anyone in particular. I have used such a system for many years and have found it to work extremely well.

A team board of directors

As you weigh delegating some of your responsibilities, you may want to consider establishing a small board of directors for the team. By selecting a group of trusted lieutenants to be headed by yourself as chairman, you will have set up a governing body to which decision-making can be partially delegated. If you have the right people, who get on well together, this can work wonderfully. However, if there is no candidate group with the right chemistry, then it is better to act alone as leader.

Deputies

Your organization will probably require you to nominate a deputy or deputies. The deputy can be used solely to deputize in your absence, with the expectation that he or she will not make major decisions. Or, your deputy can be empowered at all times and can make real decisions. Which method you choose will depend on how much you trust, and how well you can work with, your deputy.

Direct reports

Although large teams may require hierarchical levels of super-vision in order to function efficiently (as discussed more fully in the following paragraphs), it is often practical and desirable on smaller teams to have some members of the team work directly for the manager, even if only for part of their time. If you are considering this type of team structure, you might assign suitable staff members to act as your general assistants or to perform particular projects on your behalf. This approach has three beneficial effects: First, it will reduce the load on you; second, it can be useful for developing the careers of the staff who work for you; and last, staff members who work directly for you can help you understand what issues are of concern to other members of the team.

Hierarchical versus Horizontal Structures

In my view, there are two major breaking points in the size of a team. If the team contains fewer than about half a dozen peo-ple, then everyone probably will know what everyone else is doing. Once a team grows beyond this size, then it should be structured to ensure that nothing important gets dropped, and that there is sufficient communication to prevent too many mis-takes from being made.

The second breaking point occurs at about twenty-five staff members. In managing a team consisting of two-dozen or more people, you may start to feel the need to introduce at least one level of management between yourself and the rest of the team. If you have to do this, you are moving away from the type of manager this book targets. But, if you run a large team, do you really have a choice?

There are two alternative strategies for managing a large team. First, you can set up a horizontal structure. Earlier in this chapter, I described having a board of directors to help run the team. Within the board, you can dole out roles and tasks for which you, as leader, have been solely responsible, thus building a horizontal structure. You might designate one person to concentrate on sales, another to manage operations, another to handle strategy, yet another to be the creative or technical lead, and so on. Second, you could extend the horizontal structure into a hierarchical structure in which the board members would be supplemented by a group of team leaders who lead sub-teams within your team.

Administrative support

One area that is worthy of careful thought is the level of administrative support you put into your team. At one extreme, you might hire fewer support people and a greater number of value-creating staff, making people do their own photocopying, travel arrangements, and the like. Or you can go to the other extreme, bulking up the staff with administrative support personnel in order to avoid having highly paid staff doing menial tasks. My own view is that excellent support is very cost-effective, but that poor support is worse than useless.

Excellent support is very cost-effective, but poor support is worse than useless.

Consultants

We have all seen organizations that become overly dependent on management consultants. There are, however, times when bringing someone in from outside your team is appropriate:

- *An outside viewpoint is needed:* You and your team may well be basing decisions on implicit assumptions that an outsider can challenge. Outsiders will view matters dispassionately, which can help counteract the passion in yourself and the team.
- *A particular skill is needed, but on a temporary basis only:* If you are trying to build a new business opportunity in a market area that is new to your team, for example, it can be useful to hire marketing and sales consultants who have experience in the new market area, until it is clear whether or not that opportunity is going to be successful.

MEETINGS

Whole books have been written on the subject of organizing and running effective meetings—I know because I have read some of them. Rather than add to the existing literature, I have only a few salient points to make about how to conduct meetings within your team.

Determine whether a formal meeting is necessary. Not all meetings have to be formal. If someone has an urgent issue to discuss and a clear objective in mind, then he or she should consider grabbing key people for an informal meeting. In such a situation, preparatory tasks can be done on the fly, such as creating the meeting agenda on a whiteboard rather than preparing and distributing an agenda in advance.

Do not tolerate useless meetings. There is a well-known saying that warns you not to mistake movement for progress. All too often, meetings are called when there is a problem that people do not have sufficient will to tackle. If there is absolutely no will at all to tackle a problem, some genius may decide that it is necessary to set up a committee that schedules a string of meetings to look into the problem! Of course, I am being facetious here, but it does happen all too frequently that meetings get called when no positive benefit can result. Never be instrument or party to such a useless endeavor.

Insist that all meetings have a clear objective. I insist that anyone organizing a meeting answer the question, "What is the objective of this meeting?" Before calling for a meeting, the meeting's organizer should have a clear view as to what he or she would consider to be a successful outcome.

Insist that anyone arranging a meeting be fully prepared for it. The requirement that anyone calling a meeting be fully prepared for it applies to you, too! Given the pressures you and your team probably work under, it is likely that meetings are scheduled and then are not given a second thought until fifteen minutes before starting time. Because no money changes hands, it is all too easy to forget the real cost of meetings; it is your job, however, to remind people that the team must get value from its meetings. Insist that anyone arranging a meeting must do a minimum level of preparation, including, at the least, the tasks described below:

- Formulate a clear objective for the meeting.
- Prepare and distribute an agenda and any essential paperwork sufficiently in advance of the meeting to allow attendees to prepare for the meeting.
- Invite the "right" people—that is, include key people whose expertise and involvement are essential to the tasks to be discussed as well as individuals who will perform any work involved.
- Verify that key people can attend.
- Make all meeting-space arrangements well in advance— for example, by booking a room, arranging for needed equipment, and ordering meals or refreshments.

Do not tolerate long meetings. During my early days as a manager, I put a limit of one hour on all team meetings. This limitation admittedly was a bit arbitrary, but it has been my experience that meetings obey Parkinson's Law—that is, they expand to fill the time available. A time limit is one of the best ways of enforcing good chairmanship of meetings; there is nothing like a sense of dwindling time to make a chairperson run a meeting efficiently.

Verify that key people can attend meetings.

Don't feel obliged to go to every meeting. Some managers are drawn to meetings like a moth to a flame. They presumably feel that something may happen or be said at the meeting that they may need to know about. I suggest that you only go to meetings where you feel that you have something uniquely important to add.

Periodically assess the value of each regularly scheduled meeting. Meetings may not make a person feel as good as a mood-altering drug but they are just as habit-forming. To make certain that your team's meeting are more than mere habit, regularly assess the value of all meetings.

CONTROLLING THE TEAM'S FINANCES

As manager, you need to understand the specific finances of your team or project. If this is your first management position and you have no relevant financial training, there are plenty of publicly offered courses on the basics of finance, available through continuing education programs, through financial institutions, and elsewhere. In addition, if you are part of a larger organization, it is likely that your organization uses and can recommend an appropriate training course.

You need to understand the balance sheet for your team's activities. Not understanding the financial status of your team is like flying a jet, in fog, at low altitude, in the mountains, *without instruments;* it is potentially fatal. Personally, I find this aspect of a manager's job incredibly boring, but if asked whether I mind doing it, I quickly answer, "Not when you consider the alternative."

You will need to know how the numbers on the balance sheet are derived. Can you just rely on your organization's financial systems? In a word, *no.* There are a number of reasons why you should keep your own simple accounting system:

- You will want to keep your own books in order to be able to spot mistakes, such as double entries or inconsistencies, in the official figures. There is a computing term called GIGO—Garbage In, Garbage Out—that applies equally well in bookkeeping. If your balance sheet contains mistakes, then your analysis based on those figures is likely to be flawed.
- You often will need simpler figures to control your team's operations than those contained in the organization's financial systems, where it can be difficult to see the forest for the trees.
- You may sometimes need to drill down into a particular part of the figures to understand what appears to be an anomaly. Corporate systems can be frustratingly obtuse when used by the novice who is trying to find out what lies behind a particular figure.
- The organization's systems will be structured to control the financial aspects that are key to the organization, like control of cash flow, for example. Often, you will share an interest in those aspects, but will almost certainly have other requirements that your organization's systems do not support—for example, staff utilization.

Once you have the basic concepts and data that you need to control the team's finances, you can take your mastery a step further. Using the jet-airplane analogy again, ask what instruments you'll need. Work out what aspects of the finances are really important to your team's financial health and then set up your spreadsheets to monitor those aspects. Your list of highest priorities may include such factors as current and future utilization of staff, the flow of incoming orders, the money you spend on subcontractors, or cash flow and invoicing.

There are a few tips I can offer:

- Remember that GIGO applies to *your* figures, too. Cross-check your figures for internal consistency, consistency with reality (200 percent utilization is unusual), and consistency with your organization's figures.
- Don't blindly trust your spreadsheets. They are only as good as the formulae in them. It is easy to mistype numbers or to write a formula that is plausible but wrong (if tax, for example, is 15 percent, then a price with no tax is not equal to 15 percent less than the total of price with tax). It is always worth getting someone with accounting experience to check your spreadsheet design.
- If you are inexperienced, then ask someone with a background in finance to alert you to classic pitfalls (for example, not differentiating items that are exclusive of tax from those that are inclusive of tax, forgetting that everyone takes vacation in the summer, not making a realistic allowance for how long invoices take to be paid, and so on).
- Don't forget that the measure of a good set of spreadsheets is that they call your attention to problems *in good time*. This means that you will need to project your key financial indicators into the future. In order for this to work, you have to keep the data in your spreadsheets current.

A SUPPORTIVE INFRASTRUCTURE

There are a number of steps you can take to ensure that the team's activities run smoothly.

Set up a communications and computing infrastructure. Modern communications technology such as voice mail, e-mail, mobile phones, pagers, portable computers, personal agenda software, groupware, local intranets, and the like, provide immensely powerful tools for communication and interaction within your team, between your team and the rest of your organization, and between your team and its customers. This sort of technology needs to be procured, set up, used, and managed in a disciplined way if it is to deliver on its full potential.

The technology you set up constitutes a team investment that will usually repay itself many times over, but you must plan for the ongoing as well as initial investment. The ongoing investment will almost certainly require some local IT support staff—possibly just local IT-literate staff members whose main roles lie elsewhere. Even if someone is a talented IT amateur, he or she probably has many of the characteristics of professional IT staff, such as those described earlier, in Chapter 6.

One thing to be wary of is allowing IT equipment to become a status symbol. Often, the people who need the most expensive equipment have relatively low status, and you should ensure that equipment is allocated according to need.

Design lightweight processes. As noted previously, it is well worth designing a set of lightweight business processes that support, but do not stifle, the team's members.

Provide appropriate administrative support. Again as previously noted, you need to decide on an appropriate level of support for your revenue-earning staff.

Design an appropriate filing system. I do not want to go into the intricacies of the design of filing systems, but you should give thought to an appropriate design. When things go awry, well-kept files can save the team's life.

Arrange for alternative coverage during people's absences. Do you know when people will be away? Who will cover for them when they are away? Can anyone else read their e-mail and access vital computer and paper files? Do you have duplicate keys for when a key-holder is away? How well you plan for each of these situations can determine whether the team's work flows smoothly.

Design an appropriate filing system.

SUMMARY

You cannot do everything! Techniques that can help you manage better follow:

- Delegate.
- Reduce your level of perfectionism.
- Drop low-priority tasks.

Delegation is one of the hardest and most important techniques that a manager must master. You must not micromanage, but you must retain appropriate visibility and control.

You must also choose an appropriate structure for your team. I suggest you think of delegating functions and roles, rather than creating a hierarchy of sub-teams.

Although you may find it dull, you must keep a good grip on the finances of your team. Remember that your organization is likely to be unforgiving of managers who do not deliver on the bottom line.

CHAPTER 10

Managing Your Universe

Up to this point in the book, I think I can reasonably claim that in my career I have "practiced what I am preaching." Now, I must confess that I am suggesting that you "do as I say, not as I did." I offer in this chapter the hard-won experience of my own mistakes.

MANAGE YOUR MANAGERS

Your team will tend to regard itself as successful if its customers are happy with its performance. However, the team will thrive only if your managers perceive it to be a valuable part of the organization. In an ideal world, the customers' views and your managers' views would always be strongly correlated. This chapter will help you move yourself and your team toward the idealized position.

Do not get emotional. No matter how stupid, de-motivating, contradictory, and small-minded you think your managers are, *stay calm.* If you become emotional, you are as good as dead. The problem is that if you are good at your job, you are likely to be passionate about it, but you must be cool and cerebral in dealing with the rest of your organization.

Accept your boss's decisions with good grace. One of the easiest ways to annoy your boss is to continue arguing against a decision when it has been made clear to you that it will not be changed, or to sulk about a decision with which you disagree. I really wish I had realized this earlier in my career. My firm belief is that your boss is paid to make decisions, and while many bosses will allow you to make your views known, you have a duty to accept their decisions. The only exception to this rule is if you are asked to do something that is illegal or clearly against the best interests of your organization, a point I discuss further in Chapter 13, "Managing in the Real World."

You may find the following opinion radical and you may not like it: I believe that when you disagree with one of your boss's decisions, you will often be the one who has got it wrong. I say this not just because you, like me, are fallible, but also because your bosses have a broader view of the organization than you do. Often, the decision that is best for your team will not be the best from the organization's perspective. At other times, the decision you favor is simply not possible given the politics of your organization, which your bosses will understand but you may not. Even if your bosses have got it wrong, then that is their prerogative, and you will gain nothing, and risk losing the respect of your bosses, if you cannot accept their decisions with good grace.

Maintain visibility as it is the key to a good relationship with your boss. One of the best ways to keep a good working relationship with your boss is to give him or her an appropriate picture of your team's activities. In particular, give your boss as much warning as possible about problems that will become visible outside your team.

Never threaten authority. The "powers that be" will not accept explicit threats to their authority, so you need to achieve your objectives without any crude confrontations.

Accept that good teams are by their nature threatening. One of the most depressing facts about being a small team within a larger organization is that the better your team does, the more it will threaten other people and teams in the organization. The only way to tackle this is to go beyond the mere avoidance of threatening behavior and to actually be friendly to those who feel threatened. Try to get those outside the team to feel part of your success. One good way to do this is to genuinely seek advice and help from people and teams who may feel threatened.

Never, ever, threaten to resign. Just as I have advised in an earlier chapter that you not give in to threats from your key staff members, I advise you to never threaten resignation to make a point with your management. In fact, management in any sensible organization should accept the resignation of someone who threatens to leave. Threatening to resign is never the way to handle a conflict.

It is possible that you will be put in a position that is completely untenable, in which case you may have to resign. If you are unlucky enough to find yourself in this situation, just go quietly.

Remember that managerial incompetence is much more prevalent than conspiracy. It is very easy to convince yourself that the organization is out to get you and your team and that all of the annoying problems have been created intentionally rather than as a result of someone's incompetence. It is my experience that cock-ups—that's British for accidental screwups—are far more common than conspiracies. When you start seeing conspiracies behind every tree, it is best to go and have a chat with your boss, or with whoever you think is conspiring. I suggest you go in thinking the best, not the worst—whatever the problem, it is probably just the result of "normal" organizational incompetence.

Keep calling this viewpoint to the attention of your team members as there are bound to be plenty of conspiracy theorists among them. Provide a calming, rational influence, and recognize that the mood among team members will tend to be anti-establishment if they think that the organization has it in for them or for the project. Remind your team that most middle managers, personnel staff, accountants, lawyers, and the like, with whom team members must interact, tend not to be bad people, but rather are people trying to do their best under difficult circumstances. Try to be tolerant yourself, and imbue that tolerance in the team.

The mood among team members
will tend to be anti-establishment.

MANAGE YOURSELF

Do not fight battles you cannot win or that are not worth the effort. Your team may see many actions of your organization as an attempt to destroy the team's value. Occasionally, the team will be correct that there is a genuine threat, which you can try to avert by implementing some of the methods I outline below. However, there will be many battles that you either cannot win or that are not worth the effort to fight. As I have noted previously, a person can do only a few things well at any one time. Do not waste your or the team's effort on battles that you cannot win.

I followed my own advice some years ago when my organization mandated both that a particular format be used for reports and that a specific word processor be used to produce them. To say that the report format and word processor were unpopular with my team would be to understate the fact. Team members were unanimous in urging me to fight this proposal tooth and nail, but I told them that (a) we would lose, and (b) we had more important battles to win. Despite many grumbles, my view was accepted.

Know when to apply the theory of "free power." The CEO of my organization gave a good description of the philosophy that I call "the theory of free power," when he told us that

> *It is easier to ask for forgiveness than it is to ask for permission.*

It is a fact that top-level managers in most organizations do not really know how much authority they have delegated to low-level managers. So, in many cases, you can just go ahead and do things without asking in advance for approval. A significant disadvantage to acting without prior authorization, however, is that many organizations default to a blame culture, so there will be no recognition if your decision turns out well, but you will get blamed if things go wrong. In determining a course of action, decide whether you care about being blamed. If you just want to do a good job on behalf of your team and are not worried about credit or blame, you will probably use organizational free power a lot.

It may seem ingenuous, but a good technique, well backed up by personal observation and by studies conducted in the field of psychology, is to be submissive and apologetic when being blamed. It is really difficult, and certainly no fun, to beat up a groveler.

One time that I strongly recommend you consider the use of organizational free power is when the organization definitely does not want to be asked to give permission. For example, if a staff member asks your permission to do something that is not covered by the organization's rules, and the request is reasonable, just say yes. In most countries, your decision will legally bind your organization, but it eliminates the necessity that the organization itself will have to make a precedent-setting decision. In such cases, the organization will probably be much happier if you assume the local responsibility for the decision.

Copy people on your decisions. There is a middle way between asking the organization's permission and using free power. That is, you can make the decision yourself, but then copy the relevant people on your decision. Although there is the danger here that you will have your decision vetoed once it is known, your announcement makes it obvious that you are not hiding your actions.

Find the wiggle room. Within any organizational process or standard, there is nearly always room for local "interpretation." Often, it will be possible to show that your interpretation is in the spirit of the original process or instruction. When I oversaw the introduction of ISO 9001 quality processes into my team, for example, I got a copy of the actual ISO standard and showed my management that my local interpretation was directly supported by the ISO document. As my bosses' main concern was whether my process would be judged compliant by the independent standards team, they let me go my own way once I had demonstrated standards compliance to them.

Exercise your judgment. Few organizations will fire you for *not* doing things. If you find yourself faced with a job that strikes you as wrong or with instructions that you cannot obey, try to dissuade your management from following that track. As a last resort, rather than threatening to resign, look for a way around carrying out instructions to the letter. Provided you do not rub your managers' noses in the fact that you are bordering on being insubordinate, you will usually get away with it. As an example, when my organization redefined my job, I became responsible for a very time-consuming set of duties. My instructions said that I was not to delegate these duties, but I found that I had to shift some of the work to others. What did I do? I delegated the tasks but retained the ultimate responsibility for the duties myself. This splitting of tasks out from duties was definitely against the spirit of the instructions, but I saw no alternative and did what I felt I had to do. Happily, it worked out for me and the organization.

My advice to you is that you use this technique very sparingly indeed. Although your superiors may not fire you, they are likely to be able to make life very difficult for you at some time in the future.

Apologize when you have upset people. At times when I have found that my behavior or a decision has annoyed someone else in the organization, I have succeeded in defusing the situation with a strategic apology. A personal apology has usually been sufficient, but at other times, only a public apology will do. One occasion when I used a strategic apology was after I had a major row with staff in my organization's Personnel department. I lost my temper and said some regrettably unprofessional things when I felt that I was not getting proper support in a difficult case with one of my staff members. Although I believed then and still believe that I was in the right, there was no excuse for my rudeness. I needed to restore my relationship with the head of that department, and felt a personal apology was required. My apology was strategic but it also was genuine. I said that I had reacted so strongly because the particular case was very stressful and that the stress had gotten to me. I then apologized for the distress that my anger had caused. What I said was truthful—it was not an admission of guilt—and it cleared the air.

Accommodate benign neglect. There is a story that in bygone days a condemned man was being taken to the gallows to be hanged. On the way from the prison to the scaffold, the man passed the King, who was sitting on his horse. Seeing a last opportunity, the condemned man called out to the King, "In one year, I could teach your horse to speak." The King was so intrigued that he gave the man a year in which to teach his horse to talk, and then told him he possibly would be granted a pardon if he succeeded, but that he would be hanged for certain if he failed. Back in the prison, another inmate asked, "Why did you do that? All you have done is delay the inevitable." The condemned man replied, "A lot can happen in a year: The King may die, the horse may die, or the horse may learn to talk."

If you have an intractable problem with another part of the organization, then try to buy yourself some time. Intractable problems have a habit of solving themselves. Too often, managers panic and provoke an unnecessary crisis or confrontation when leaving matters to heal with time would better suit their purpose.

Ask for assistance. When dealing with people in other departments, such as Personnel or Finance, appeal to their professional pride in how well they know the ins and outs of their job by asking them for advice on ways to accomplish something outside the normal rules. If you seek assistance from someone who has this kind of professional pride, he or she will often tell you where the wiggle room is.

Going a step further, if you develop a good relationship with a particular person, then your dealings with his or her department can be transformed. One way to help develop such a relationship is to be courteous and appreciative, for example by thanking someone for doing a good job.

Know when you need a specialist's help. As the lowest level of manager in an organization, a front-line manager is a bit like a family doctor: He or she is the first line of defense when a problem crops up. The good family doctor knows immediately when a problem needs to be referred to a specialist; likewise, the good manager must be alert to problems that should be referred to a senior manager, Personnel, or the Legal department. If you find yourself facing such a situation, ask yourself, "How badly could this all go?" For example, if there is even the remotest chance that your organization could end up in the news or in court, I strongly suggest you seek expert help.

Tap into the support subculture. Secretaries and support staff of all kinds can be a valuable source of information and help for you as a front-line manager in your dealings with the rest of the organization. If you apply my advice about being courteous to your team members to people outside your team, then you will find it relatively easy to tap into the support subculture. You will find that stopping for a chat with secretaries and support staff is not only interesting, it can be very informative. Such people often have some power to help you, and always have great power to hinder you.

MANAGE OFFICE POLITICS

I really, really wish I could honestly say that you should take no notice of office politics. Unfortunately, I think that approach is as fatal as it is naïve. People on your team will be aware that others in the organization play at office politics, and they need to be confident that you can handle the heat. Several recommendations deserve elaboration, as described below.

Don't use politics to attack other people. If you take advantage of office politics to attack someone, I hope the person or people you attack manage to repay you in kind—my point here being that such attacks invite retaliation. You may have to compete with your colleagues for resources or a promotion, but it is my opinion that the smartest move is to play hard but fair.

What should you do if someone attacks you? I know of four possible responses, of which only the first three can be recommended:

1. *Retreat:* If conflict is unavoidable and you are unlikely to win, or the issue is not important enough to warrant conflict, then the wisest course of action can be to withdraw. Withdrawal may be taken as a sign of weakness, but in the right circumstances, a strategic retreat can make a lot of sense.
2. *Neither retreat nor retaliate:* The advantage of standing your ground without taking retaliatory action is that it gives you and your team the moral edge. The main disadvantage of this approach is that it may encourage further attacks because people will see you as a soft target. In my view, the advantages often outweigh the disadvantages, but if you cannot stomach this approach, then I recommend the next response.
3. *Respond to the attack, retaliating with a similar level of force as the attacker used on you and your team:* Your managers are unlikely to think that you are behaving unreasonably if you carry out a retaliation that is in proportion

197

to the attack you've suffered, but you may be seen to be behaving no better than the attacker. There is a danger that your retaliation will provoke further attacks, but it may defeat the attack and deter others from similar attacks.

4. *Respond to the attack using an escalated level of force:* I cannot recommend this course of action and must warn you that your managers will probably feel that you are overreacting. You are also likely to provoke a further attack unless you have destroyed the attacker. The potential benefit is that your massive retaliation may well deter any other attacker.

Respond using an escalated level of force.

There is a saying that "revenge is a dish best served cold." If you are attacked, it is likely that at some later date you will find yourself in a position to pay back the attacker. Should you take such an opportunity? All I can tell you is that I always try to resist the temptation, . . . and sometimes I succeed.

Understand organizational politics to sell your ideas. When you want to sell an idea to your organization, you need to understand how to present your views in a way that the organization will find attractive. At any time, your organization will have "hot buttons" you need to press, and "cold buttons" you need to avoid pressing. The only way to find out what is in favor, and what is out of favor, is to be aware of the political climate outside your team.

Build power relationships in your organization. Is it worth fighting a battle you cannot win? There may be rare circumstances when the morale of your team requires that you fight, even though you know you are likely to lose. Generally speaking, however, the name for a person who fights battles that he or she is likely to lose is "fool."

Often, you will only be able to win if you have powerful allies. Remember that the best way to gain allies is to be valuable to them. This is one way in which behavior that is good for your organization can also be good for your team.

Know what the organization will reward and punish. Some of your incentives will be explicit, but many of your incentives (and disincentives) will be implicit in the political structure of your organization. You need to be constantly aware that you do well if, and only if, your organization perceives that you have done well. Likewise, you have done badly if you are perceived to have done badly.

MANAGE ORGANIZATIONAL INITIATIVES

Today's organizations generally seem keen on buzzword-based initiatives, and require managers to deal daily with such concepts as knowledge management, total quality, reengineering, benchmarking, and the like. In addition, managers must contend with sometimes daunting annual tasks, such as those connected with budgets and strategic business planning, which seem to change their form each year. How does one handle them? There are a number of ways for front-line managers to handle initiatives, some of my favorites of which are suggested later in this section.

Before discussing these techniques, however, it is worth noting two situations that pose a particular danger. If you have either a new CEO or an especially outstanding CEO, then it is likely that anyone who is viewed as not fully embracing a corporate initiative may face considerable risk to his or her career. In these situations, you will want to be seen as being energetic in your implementation of organizational initiatives.

Be first—or last. There can be an advantage to being first to embrace an initiative. First off, you probably will earn brownie points. Second, you probably will also have the maximum say in setting the interpretation of the initiative. If neither of these "benefits" seems likely, let other people get all the bugs out and take up the initiative at the last possible moment.

Hijack the initiative. Initiatives often come with some sort of funding, even if it is only some allowance of time for you and your staff. Consider whether you can use the initiative to make a change that you wanted to make anyway. For example, you might do what many people do and use the introduction of quality processes to reengineer a slicker set of procedures for managing business within the team.

The great advantage of such an approach is that the team is likely to be more motivated in implementing the initiative if there is some direct benefit to the team. It is my view that the skillful manager can turn almost all initiatives to some advantage, thereby avoiding the difficult situation in which he or she must try to get the team to implement an unpopular initiative.

Use the initiative to negotiate a change in your sales or deliverables targets. It is often possible to use an initiative to negotiate a change to your existing targets with your boss. Your boss may well accept that the new priority implied by the latest initiative means that existing priorities have to be reassessed.

Do initiatives well enough. Avoid the mistake of overdoing the level of effort to implement an initiative. If you put it positively, stating that you are looking to get the maximum "bang for the buck" from the initiative, this will not be seen as a criticism of the initiative.

MANAGE PERSONAL GOALS, REWARDS, AND TARGETS

Personal targets and goals are dangerous. Your staff will know that upper management probably has set targets for you to meet and will suspect, often correctly, that you are allowing the pursuit of your bonus to affect your decisions. There are some steps you can take to manage these dangers.

Be open about your targets and bonuses. I cannot think of any better way to defuse the suspicions of your team than being totally open. I suggest that you acknowledge that the smart thing for the team and for you to do is to keep the organization happy by hitting as many of the targets as possible. Targets are often incremental, and it is usually possible to achieve them without doing significant damage to other related performance indicators. If pursuing a target could damage more worthwhile goals that you and the team share, discuss with the team the extent to which you should balance each target against the other more important factors. You cannot ignore the organization's targets, no matter how stupid you believe them to be, but if you are clever enough, you will be able to reach them in such a way as to keep your integrity and show your professionalism.

Share your bonuses. In a previous chapter, I recommended that you use part of any bonus you receive to sponsor team social events. The idea bears repeating here—after all, it is largely due to the efforts of your staff members that you are rewarded.

SUMMARY

The six ideas I would like you to take away from this chapter follow:

1. Do not get emotional with your bosses. Passion is a great attribute of a manager and leader, but can turn out to be a terrible way to deal with the rest of your organization.

2. Accept your bosses' decisions with good grace.
3. Give your bosses a clear view of what is going on in your team.
4. Use the "free power" within the organization, recognizing that it is sometimes better to apologize after the event than to ask for permission beforehand.
5. Find the wiggle room within your organization's processes, in part by building a good working relationship with people in such other departments as Finance, Legal, and Personnel.
6. Try to use your organization's initiatives to implement improvements within your team.

CHAPTER 11

Managing People Outside
Your Organization

In the previous chapter, my subject matter was broadly concerned with internal politics and offered techniques for managing people inside your own organization. In this chapter, I address the critically important people issues involved in the business relationships you must develop outside your organization. By outside, I mean customers, suppliers, partners, foreigners, and the like.

Of all the business relationships you need to develop with outsiders, the single most important one is with your customers.

CUSTOMERS

One concept discussed previously is key to establishing a productive relationship with your customers and involves what they perceive to be fact. Stated simply,

It is the customers' perceptions that matter, not the reality.

What this means, of course, is that if your customers perceive that the quality of your product or service is inadequate, then you have a problem, regardless of the actual quality of the product or service. This business-related problem with quality is also a people-related problem, and applies to all aspects of your dealings with your customers, from products to services to responsiveness—in short, everything. Rather than complaining that the customers have the wrong perceptions, understand that it is your actions—and sometimes even your inaction—that have allowed the wrong perceptions to take hold, and it now is your job to better market yourself and your team in order to change those perceptions.

Although caring for customers is not a humorous matter, there are a number of amusing rules for customer care. My favorite set follows:

Rule 1: The customer is always right.
Rule 2: When the customer is wrong, refer to Rule 1.

A very important rule for good customer care is, *Never give the customer an unpleasant surprise.* The key word in this rule is *surprise.* Most customers accept that things will go wrong, and a large part of a customer's trust in a supplier comes from the way in which the supplier handles those inevitable problems.

When you, as manager, first find out that there is a problem, it is tempting to try to correct the problem so that the customer never finds out. The trouble is, once things have started to go wrong, they usually get worse before they get better. In most cases, the better tactic is to let the customer know what the problem is and then discuss what you are doing to handle the problem. When you are dealing with a problem, the first and most important thing to realize is, *Problems provide great opportunities for improving your relationship with a customer.*

Because most customers accept that things will go wrong, they truly appreciate a supplier who handles problems well. There is a story, possibly apocryphal, about an automobile manufacturer that admitted that it did not necessarily aim for zero defects in its cars. The executive being interviewed is reported to have said, "The best number of defects-under-warranty is one—handled brilliantly by the dealer."

When there is a problem, you need to get yourself out of the mind-set of "oh no, we have screwed up," and into the mind-set of "now I have a chance to impress the customer."

There can be an important role for you as manager to play personally in sorting out a customer complaint. A personal call or, in a serious situation, a personal visit from The Boss can send a very positive message about the importance you attach to the relationship with that customer.

Problems provide great opportunities for improving your relationship with a customer.

Give the customer the worst-case estimate for solving a problem. At first glance, this rule appears to be counterintuitive and seems to contradict the point that I made previously. Having screwed up, a manager's natural tendency is to attempt to minimize the customer's perception of the severity of the problem and to impress the customer with how fast the problem can be sorted out. To do this, you will be tempted to quote the minimum possible time for fixing the problem, which is a big mistake.

Consider the following scenario: Your party arrives at a restaurant at 9:25 P.M. for a 9:30 reservation. You are told that your table will not be ready until 9:45 and you are asked whether you would like to wait in the bar. You agree, and settle in at the bar, still waiting as 9:45 comes and goes. At 10 P.M., you are told that your table is ready.

Now consider a slightly different scenario: Your party arrives at a restaurant at 9:25 P.M. for a 9:30 reservation. The restaurant manager apologetically tells you that there is a problem; he explains that your reservation is for the second sitting at Table 5 and that the guests from the first sitting are running late. Expressing doubt that your table will be ready before 10:15, the manager again apologizes and offers you complimentary drinks while you wait. You agree, and settle in at the bar. At 10 P.M., the manager comes to you to say that the restaurant has moved the first group to have complimentary coffee in the bar and that your table is now ready.

I hope you do not need convincing that the second scenario is much likelier than the first to transform an irritated customer into a happy camper. I have been to a (very) few restaurants that practice the second technique, but the number that practice the first tells me that this customer-care technique is not as well known as it should be.

You may have noticed that I slipped a couple of other customer-care techniques into the restaurant example, perhaps the most important of which is, *When there is a problem, be open and honest with the customer.*

In the second scenario, the restaurant manager immediately describes the precise nature of the problem and then, upon resolution of the problem, explains the way it was solved faster than had been expected. A general rule for good customer management is to be open and honest with your customers, but when there is a problem, understand that openness and honesty are mandatory, never optional.

A second customer-care technique depicted in the restaurant scenario is, *Apologize, explain—but do not blame others or make excuses.*

In the story, the manager reports that the first customers are running late, but he does not try to blame them, for example by saying that they arrived late. Even if the first customers were at fault, the manager should not try to blame them. After all, the manager could have turned late arrivals away rather than risk their encroaching on the second sitting. What I am trying to emphasize with this story is that the best start to rectifying the situation is to assume full responsibility and accept full blame.

When there is a problem, be willing to offer sweeteners to your customer. In the second scenario above, the manager offered the inconvenienced customers complimentary drinks at the bar. The technique of offering something gratis to offset a service failure should already be known to you, but if not, here's the premise: When you screw up with a customer, you have in effect broken either an explicit or implicit contract between yourself and the customer. If you are a sensible businessperson, then the price at which you sold your product or service contained a contingency for exactly such eventualities. It is human nature not to offer up your profit margin without being asked to, but often the best way to turn a disaster into a public-relations triumph is an honest apology and a thoughtful offer of something free to help compensate for the problem. Notice that I encouraged "a thoughtful offer"—in a restaurant, for example, an offer of free drinks or a bottle of wine may be better received than an offer to deduct money from the bill. The fact that the customer will probably value drinks at the purchase price listed on the bar menu, rather than at the price the restaurant actually pays its wholesalers, means that "thoughtful" can be cheaper for the service provider as well as more appreciated by the customer.

Some years ago, I encountered an impressive display of "thoughtful" customer care when I arrived at a Washington, D.C., hotel after a very long flight—only to find that the hotel had lost my reservation. Distinctly annoyed, I stood mutely at the reservations desk—but before I could open my mouth to complain, the reservations clerk said, "It's totally our problem and we will correct it. We should have a room for you within the hour, but if we do not, our limo will move you to a more expensive hotel where you will only pay our rate. For now, I can store your luggage if you would like to wait in the restaurant and have a meal on us." Rather than remain angry, I ended up thanking the clerk profusely, and I always make a point of staying in the same hotel chain whenever I can.

One important point about the hotel incident is that I doubt that the clerk's excellent handling of my problem happened by accident. That reservations clerk had been carefully trained to handle a potential customer-relations nightmare. It is your job, as manager, to make sure your staff members are properly trained to react in the most positive way to such problems.

If a customer refuses to calm down, remain calm and submissive yourself. This piece of advice reminds me of the two humorous rules I gave at the start of this section: The customer is always right—even when he or she is wrong. Even if you follow *all* the rules I have outlined so far, there will still be some customers who choose not to be placated. The most common reason for this is that customers who cannot be reasoned with are not reasonable people, but under no circumstances whatsoever is it the right thing to point out the unreasonableness or illogicality of their position.

If a customer refuses to calm down,
remain calm and submissive yourself.

Throughout this chapter, I have consistently maintained that honesty is the best policy, but advocating honesty in this case would be a lie: Being open and honest does not work with customers who refuse to calm down. Remain submissive and apologetic, look dejected at your failure to make a valued customer happy, and ask what you can do that would satisfy him or her. You may find that you have the authority to do what the customer asks, or you may want to say that you will have to discuss the complaint with a more senior person.

Tell your customers not to bottle up their problems. Encouraging your customers to discuss problems they have with you, your staff, or the service or products you supply is a similar technique to one I have recommended in dealing with your staff. By letting your customers know that you openly solicit criticism, you make it less likely that they will bottle up their complaints until they finally explode and take their business away. I have known managers who go so far as to give all customers their phone number, suggesting that customers call them directly if there is a problem.

Remember that honesty is nearly always profitable (in the long term). Genuine honesty is a beguiling quality in a service provider or supplier. However, honesty can actually cost you profit and business in the short term. Charging a reasonable price even when your products are in great demand, for example, may result in the short-term loss of profit. Likewise, giving honest estimates of delivery times can cause you to lose business to less scrupulous suppliers who over-claim and then under-deliver so as to appear (initially) more attractive in the eyes of their customers. Making extravagant promises about your products and under-delivering on those promises is a recipe for long-term failure. So, the next time you think about using any of these unscrupulous tactics, remember that although doing so may boost your short-term profits, honesty will always reap greater benefits in the long run.

*Making extravagant promises about your products
is a recipe for long-term failure.*

GENERAL ISSUES

At the beginning of the previous discussion, I noted that customers probably are the most important of all outsiders with
whom a front-line manager and his or her team must interact.
In my view, suppliers form the next most important group of
outsiders. However, before the discussion moves on to suppliers, let's look at some of the difficulties and challenges posed
by different categories of outsider.

Balance of Power

When dealing with people outside your organization, you
almost always must consider the balance of power in those
relationships. With customers, the balance of power is usually
weighted in their favor. Because customers pay the piper, they
usually call the tune. Many readers will be able to identify
with the manager whose customer requested that he dance
naked in the street with a rose in his teeth. The request
prompted the response, "What color rose?" The good news
here is that when dealing with suppliers, *you* are the customer,

and the balance of power will usually be weighted heavily in your favor.

The balance of power in other relationships may be far less clear. For example, in dealing with partners, think carefully about the relative strengths of your position vis-à-vis the other party. One important issue is how dependent each party is on the other. Once you start thinking in these terms, you may realize that even the relationship of customer to supplier is not as simple as you might imagine. For example, if you are working for a customer, how badly do you need his or her business? Remember that relationships tend to follow what is called the 80:20 rule, also known as Pareto's Law, which predicts that 80 percent of your revenue will come from just 20 percent of your customers. If the customer is in the top 20 percent of your customers, he or she does have significant power to hurt you by taking the business elsewhere.

Although predictable in certain situations, the balance of power in a relationship is seldom static. For example, if you are one of the first customers a supplier has, then you will be extremely important. If you remain a customer, then you will retain some residual loyalty, but your importance will decline with time. In many relationships, the balance of power can flip over so that the most powerful party in the relationship changes around.

There are many instances of this shift in power—in business, in sports, and in life—but one recent experience I had illustrates my point: As a first-time book author in search of a publisher, I quickly learned that a prospective publisher holds most of the power cards in the partnership. With no established track record, I could demand only just so much. However, were this book to become the best-seller I dream it will, then I would expect that I will hold the trump cards for my second book. Whether it is a seller's or a buyer's market determines who has the power in most partnerships, as will be discussed more fully later in this chapter.

In dealing with customers, ask yourself whether there is anything you can do to mitigate the lack of power you have as supplier in the relationship. One very successful technique is to give the relationship a personal face. At its best, putting a personal face on a business relationship will help the customer to identify with your team. In such situations, you generally can be very open with the customer about your problems and aspirations, with the result that the customer may actively help you solve your problems (by relaxing an unforgiving deadline, for example) and achieve your aspirations (perhaps by serving as a business reference).

The Culture Clash

In addition to the issue of the balance of power, there is a second key issue regarding relationships with people outside your organization: I call it the *culture clash.* I have mentioned the power of developing a personal relationship with key individuals in the customer organization, but I must warn you now to be cognizant of the fact that the behavior of individuals is conditioned by the organizational culture in which they work. There is plenty of opportunity for problems when the culture of the customer organization differs substantially from your organization's and your team's culture. For example, imagine that the customer organization has a heavyweight quality-process culture, and that you work in a much less formal environment. In such a situation, you will need to ensure that the customer is comfortable that you are giving enough attention to the quality of the product or service you are providing.

Time invested in understanding the customer's culture is usually time well spent. Not only does such study help you to spot mismatches, such as quality-process cultures, but it also will enable you to better understand the environment in which the customer operates. Find out as much as possible about the power relationships and politics within your customers' organizations. Knowing what will make your customers look good within their organizations allows you to do things that will delight your customers. As specific details of your dealings with customers fade in their memories, recollections of how you delighted them are the most likely to remain.

SUPPLIERS

There is a lot you can do to foster good relationships with your suppliers—in fact, you can apply many of the techniques I have recommended above for dealing with customers—but the first question you need to ask is, "Is it worth the effort?" I expect that you may ignore much of my advice about not working excessively long hours but, even if you do work very long hours, there is no way you can do everything well that you would like, so you need to be sure that effort spent on relationships with suppliers is well spent. Ask yourself the following question: Does the supplier offer some unique capability, or are there lots of plug-compatible alternate sources of supply? If the answer is that there are plenty of alternate sources of supply, then I suggest you ration the amount of time you invest in your relationship with that supplier.

There are a number of useful techniques for managing suppliers, some of which may require you to behave in ways that are not natural to you, especially if you are a pleasant, easygoing sort of person. These tactics are described below.

Be demanding as demanding customers often get better service. Just think of your own relationships with your customers. Go on, be honest. You give more attention to the demanding customers than you do to the nice ones, don't you? Personally, I would recommend that you be demanding but reasonable, although I have to say that being unreasonable does not seem to do much harm. It is just that being unreasonable seems to me to be unnecessarily unpleasant.

Beware of making friends with your suppliers. When I discussed dealing with customers in a previous section, I suggested that you try to form a personal relationship with your customers. I now suggest that when you are the customer, you be wary of getting involved in a personal relationship with the supplier. The reason for this is that you will often find yourself needing to register complaints with suppliers—that's the nature of being the customer for someone else's product or service. So, unless you are comfortable saying things like, "This has nothing to do with our friendship, but I am really unhappy with . . . " then avoid becoming friends in the first place.

Give both positive and negative feedback to suppliers. Just as you need to give your staff appropriate praise and constructive criticism, you will also need to give suppliers appropriate feedback on their performance. Many people find it hard to give suppliers constructive criticism, but both your suppliers and you will benefit from well-thought-out feedback.

Pay your invoices promptly. I have been pretty hard-nosed about the way you should handle your suppliers. There is, however, one issue where I am fully on the supplier's side, and that is the issue of payment. More good companies have failed because of cash-flow problems than almost anything else I can think of. I believe that it is your duty to pay your suppliers as promptly as practical. Interestingly, prompt payment is not just an issue of what is right to do; it can also be good business: You can get real benefit from being a good payer. Suppliers want business from good payers, and will often be more amenable to being squeezed on price by a customer they know pays their invoices promptly. Paying promptly also provides a useful point to bring up when you are asking for better service: "I may be demanding, but I always pay my bills on time" is a very powerful line to take.

PARTNERS

I like to define partners as those people you work with to some mutual benefit. Partners may be organizations you collaborate with to produce products or services, channels through which you market your products and services, or fellow travelers in some collaborative endeavor—for example, political lobbyists or joint prosecutors in some legal action.

It is my opinion that a partnership is the hardest of all business relationships to get right. Some of the causes of problems I have encountered are detailed below.

The two parties lend unequal importance to the relationship. If one organization or party is significantly more dependent on the relationship than the other, this almost always leads to friction, with the more dependent partner constantly nagging the less dependent organization to take on more than the latter wants.

I wish I had some truly sage advice to offer for handling this situation, but all I can do is suggest that if you analyze the partnership beforehand and find that it falls into this category, then only get involved if you are willing to deal with the inevitable friction. The best thing you can do is to talk openly with the other party before the partnership starts and try to agree about what each party can expect of the other.

The balance of power changes. A change in the balance of power between partners can be particularly unsettling, and seems to be more common in certain industries than in others. Perhaps as a first-time book author, I have a heightened appreciation of the potential for change in the balance of power between author and publisher or author and agent, with the author accumulating more power as his or her work becomes known—or so I like to imagine. I have, however, encountered this situation a number of times in my business career, so I think it is a situation that may not be uncommon.

The most severe situations that I have encountered are when one partner has lost power precipitously. If you find yourself in such a situation, do not make the following two classic mistakes.

- *Do not depend on the loyalty of the other party to keep the partnership afloat.* If you find yourself on the sorry end of a power shift, for example, facing a partner to whom you gave a first break, you may think that your partner should be grateful to you forever. Think again. Played carefully, loyalty can be a powerful factor in a relationship, but try pushing it too far and not only will it cease to have the desired effect, it can often lead to feelings of exploitation.

- *Do not depend on a legal contract, signed before the balance of power changed, to keep the partnership healthy.* This may sound like very strange advice. After all, contracts are thought by many to be sacrosanct, but such thinking reflects unfounded optimism. It is my view that contracts both should set down details with which both parties to an ongoing relationship are comfortable and also should describe how the parties will part if the relationship collapses. If the balance of power changes and the newly powerful partner does not want to abide by the terms of the contract, then the relationship is likely to break down. In such a situation, no contract on earth will keep a relationship going.

By avoiding the preceding two mistakes, you may be able to successfully manage a change in the balance of power, but what else can you do? First, when structuring a contract for a partnership, anticipate the likelihood of a change in power and restrict the time or domain of applicability. The contract could prescribe how terms will alter as the power changes or it could allow for renegotiation once certain conditions have been met. Second, include a provision that enables the newly weaker party to renegotiate the contract in order to preserve a relationship that both sides are happy to live with. Without this provision, the weaker party too frequently insists on sticking to the letter of the initial contract and ends up losing everything.

FOREIGNERS

For this discussion, I deliberately chose the emotive title *Foreigners,* rather than a more politically correct title such as *People from Different Cultures,* to try to highlight the great problems that you may encounter when dealing with people from different cultural backgrounds. The first difficulty may stem from the issue of language.

English Speakers, Beware!

Native English speakers have a great advantage in the business world, as English is the de facto lingua franca of international business, and also of the Internet. There are, however, many pitfalls awaiting English speakers, as described in the paragraphs below.

It's easy to offend non-English speakers. If you are doing business in a non-English-speaking country, then it is essential to be sensitive about assuming that English will be used in meetings. A colleague of mine has a wonderful phrase for this kind of mistake, calling it committing *assumicide*. There are a number of techniques that can help:

- Always ask in advance if it is acceptable to use English. An apologetic explanation, such as one stating that you are bringing in a top expert who only speaks English, will often help. This explanation is important because it will then be clear that you are not assuming that speaking only English is okay.
- If it is agreed that English will be used, ask how well the various participants understand and can speak English, and ensure that you converse with participants in a way that is appropriate to their fluency in English. This will show that you are both professional and polite.
- Speak slowly and clearly and avoid colloquialisms. Keep sentences short and try not to use different words to describe the same thing. These techniques are difficult to master and so it is worth having each member of your team watch the others to signal if anyone is in danger of not being understood. Be aware as well that humor often does not cross the language divide and is usually best avoided.
- If possible, take along someone who is a native speaker of the non-English language who can act as interpreter if necessary. Such a person can also help smooth over any cultural gaffes you might make.
- Learn enough of the foreign language to say "good morning," "please," and "thank you," but seek local advice regarding expected and accepted behavior.

Remember to use the techniques described above when dealing with a non-English-speaking member of your own staff.

Even if you are talking to a person of another English-speaking culture, you should be aware that many words may have different meanings in different countries or even in different locales within the same country. Also, you need to remember that colloquial or idiomatic usage may not be understood.

Cultural Differences

At a superficial level, the world is becoming more homogeneous as many aspects of Western culture spread to other countries. Do not let a superficial similarity between countries fool you into ignoring the deep differences between cultures and the way people conduct business. Areas in which it is very easy to commit assumicide include

- what is considered polite and what is considered rude
- what is considered respectful and disrespectful
- what is considered offensive
- how much physical personal space an individual will be comfortable with
- how meetings are handled (in the East versus the West, for example)
- what is considered acceptable business practice
- personal habits
- attitudes toward women
- acceptability of some jokes
- eating conventions
- religious issues
- attitudes toward alcohol consumption in social settings
- different interpretations of body language
- the giving and receiving of presents

The most intelligent way to avoid assumicide is to find someone in your community or organization from the culture you must deal with, and get that person to brief you on relevant cultural issues. It may also be worth trying to get someone from the local culture to monitor you and your team members in cross-cultural meetings.

SUMMARY

Customers

Don't give your customers unpleasant surprises. When something unpleasant does happen, you must see that problem as an opportunity to impress your customer. In recovering from a problem, it is best to under-promise and over-deliver. It is a good technique to try to make friends with your customers.

Suppliers

Don't let suppliers make a friend of you! It may be sad to acknowledge, but demanding customers get the best service.

Partners

Partnerships can be difficult when one side is much more dependent on the relationship than the other. You must be very aware when the balance of power in a relationship changes significantly. If you find that you have lost a lot of power, do not rely on a contract to save you; it may be best to renegotiate a contract to reflect your weakened position.

Foreigners

Do not allow the fact that the world appears to be becoming more homogeneous to blind you to the very large differences between cultures. Be especially wary if you are a native speaker of English. Do not assume that everyone is happy to always use English in meetings. If you are talking to non-English speakers, then remember your manners and speak slowly and clearly, without using colloquialisms. Seek advice from someone from the local culture.

CHAPTER 12

Revisiting Common Management Themes

Although this chapter is not the final one in the book, I use it to provide a summary of the book's underlying themes, which are the foundation for the practical, real-world scenarios presented in the next chapter.

MANAGING DEPENDENCIES

Throughout this book, I have focused on different aspects of management viewed in isolation, but, as a manager in the real world, you will need to consider them as a whole. What this means is that your leadership style must be appropriate to the culture you are creating. The team's culture must be appropriate both to the business you are in and to the customers to whom you sell products and services. Your business must fit your team's capabilities. Your team's organization and processes must fit the culture and your business. The team's culture must be matched to your organization's culture. Your recruitment process must match the organization's culture and business needs, and so on.

Managing these dependencies well is one of the characteristics that separate the great manager from the merely competent manager. In the following paragraphs, I address all-important qualities such as vision, integrity, passion, courage, respect, fair play, focus, and the like.

Vision Revisited

I hope I have made it clear that I regard the people-oriented aspects of a *manager's* job to be very important, but I do not kid myself that they are the most important aspects of a *leader's* job. In my opinion, the single most important role a leader has is to know where his or her team is going—that is, the leader's vision of the future. In your role as leader, never let all the pressures on you squeeze out your most important task, which is to create a sound, challenging, and easily comprehendible business strategy. Once you have such a strategy, you need to communicate it to your staff, so that team members adopt your vision as their vision.

The Golden Rule

Your own personal behavior sets the example that your team will follow. There is no way I can overemphasize the importance of this Golden Rule. It does not matter how well you can talk the talk, what matters is that you can walk the walk. The power of the Golden Rule comes into its own if you have strong principles on which to base your actions.

Integrity Revisited

Management is so much easier if you want to use your position to make things you strongly believe in happen. It is also much easier if you have a clear view of right and wrong. If you have a strong moral foundation on which to base your behavior, you can behave naturally—and, because the right behavior comes naturally to you, you also will behave consistently.

In the chapter on leadership, I suggested that managers should consider faking good behavior in situations in which the right behavior does not seem to come naturally. The reason I gave this advice is that I believe that doing the "right thing" is nearly always the smart thing, even when it is calculated rather than natural behavior. I have seen this approach adopted many times and have come to the conclusion that most people

DR. PEELING'S PRINCIPLES OF MANAGEMENT

can deduce what the right thing is in most circumstances. The Golden Rule of Management will ensure that those managers who behave in a principled way will be respected. Staff members will not respect you less—and may even respect you more—if they know that you are using your intellect rather than your nature to behave well.

The straight bat

Another example of the application of integrity is to use what I call the straight-bat approach to tricky management problems. The phrase "straight bat" comes from cricket and denotes someone who plays a straightforward shot, and does not try to do anything clever. In situations in which you are unsure what people's motives or reactions will be, I recommend that you take a principled view of trying to do the right thing. There are three advantages to taking this approach: First, behaving according to your principles is as effective as, and often more effective than, utilizing sophisticated tactics. Second, it is very easy to defend your actions when you believe strongly in them. Third, if your approach does not solve whatever tricky management problem you face and you end up getting hammered, then, at the least, you can console yourself with the thought that you tried to do the right thing and that your problems are not the result of playing politics or behaving badly.

Passion Revisited

It is my conviction that the passionate pursuit of a vision is what distinguishes a leader from a manager. In most circumstances, passion is a very positive attribute of a leader and is one of the most powerful motivators for a team. There is, however, a downside of which the passionate leader must be aware: Passionate people can become overly emotional in circumstances in which the more dispassionate person can remain cool and detached. There are times when the cool and detached approach is essential—for example, when needing to cut one's losses, and when dealing with your superiors.

MANAGING EXTREMES

Managers must accept that they will have to respond in extreme ways, and the best managers learn to utilize the extremes of both passion and detachment. Previously, I described how managers may need to react very hard and very fast to some situations, whereas in other cases, they will be best served by a policy of benign neglect. Whether demonstrating qualities of leadership, cultivating team culture, or mastering people-management, managers and leaders must consider adopting extreme and courageous positions. Clearly, management is not a job for the faint-hearted.

Courage Revisited

Have the courage to confront problems. A common failing in otherwise good managers is the lack of courage to face problems. Managers are paid to make decisions, and they need to make decisions both when they are directly faced with problems and also when they know that there is a serious problem lurking beneath the surface.

Have the courage to be ruthless. Earlier in the book, I recommended mixing the extremes of kindness and ruthlessness in areas such as people-management. This bit of advice relates to a second common failing I see in otherwise outstanding managers: They are too kind. It is my view that kindness inappropriately applied can in reality be cruel and bad management. Take, for example, a seemingly kind decision to keep a long-term under-performer on your team. Someone who is under-performing is quite likely unhappy; most people like to do a good job and to be appreciated. That person might well be under-performing because he or she does not fit into your team or has little talent for the assigned task. Such a person is a danger to the long-term survival of the team, and other members of your staff are likely to suffer increased pressure as a result of covering for the under-performer's lack of performance. All in all, your behavior in this situation may make everyone unhappy, so your kindness, in truth, may have more to do with a lack of courage on your part than with an act of kindness.

Respect, Fair Play, and Courtesy

Although I encourage you to consider extreme or ruthless behavior when appropriate, such extremes of behavior must be counterbalanced with behavior that is consistent, fair-minded, respectful, and courteous. Not only is such behavior right, it is also smart. A courteous request usually achieves more than a curt command. Fair-mindedness and consistency will allow ruthless behavior to be applied appropriately, without creating a climate of fear.

MANAGING YOURSELF

I have alluded a number of times to the extreme pressures under which most front-line managers work. You look after your staff, but who looks after you? It may be that you have a relationship with a supportive boss who helps you decide what actions to take, or you may have organized your team to have a few trusted lieutenants who can act as a support group. However, if you have no one who is looking after your welfare, then you have a duty to look after yourself.

There is a great danger that your response to pressure will be to regularly work very long hours. I have fallen into this trap myself and when I eventually broke the habit of working excessively long hours, I was able to see how disastrous, for me as well as for those around me, the pattern had been:

- I was so tired that my judgment was severely impaired.
- I worked less efficiently than when I reduced my working hours.
- I overlooked essential activities, neglecting intra- and interdepartmental communication and long-term planning.
- I lost the ability to say no, taking on more work and attending more meetings than I should have.

- I set a bad example for my team, whose members started to copy my work patterns.
- I grew progressively ill-tempered and moody.
- I neglected my home life, which suffered very badly.

If you have the long-hours habit, try an experiment: Cut your hours and see whether things improve for you as dramatically as they did for me.

Focus

The three most important techniques for making good decisions are focus, focus, and yes, . . . focus! The ability to focus is important for most people but is doubly useful to a front-line manager who probably can count on achieving only a few objectives in any given period of time. For example, only a few of the goals identified in a business strategy can be achieved in a year; a team can expect to be outstanding in only a few areas; and you can only win a few battles with your management. By picking your goals carefully and focusing on them, you stand a better chance of achieving them.

Play to your strengths. A common mistake many front-line managers make is they seek to achieve an idealized situation. You have to work with what you have at hand. It is no good pretending that you are proficient at things at which you are inadequate; it is much better to delegate those tasks to someone with more talent. In this way, you can develop a leadership style that makes the most of your abilities, while minimizing the damage done by your weaknesses. You need to organize your team around the staff you actually have, deploying people on jobs that play to their talents.

Do not mix delegation and micromanagement. Most managers know the importance of delegation, but few managers understand how to delegate properly. Choosing what jobs to delegate, to whom, with an up-front agreement as to the level of control over the delegated task, have been discussed in some detail in previous chapters. The need to allow people to do things differently from yourself, and the need to let people learn from their mistakes, make delegation one of the hardest tasks a manager will face. You have to let go of detailed control, while remaining in overall control. Unless you demonstrate your trust that your staff members can work well without detailed supervision, they will never develop the confidence and experience to be worthy of your trust.

PERCEPTIONS ARE THE ONLY REALITY

Marketing people should understand the maxim that perceptions are the only reality, but it is important that you, as a frontline manager, also understand the concept, for it applies to all your activities. For example, if you are perceived as being unfair, then whether you are or are not fair is unimportant; you must address the perception. Do not make the mistake of blaming anyone other than yourself for wrong perceptions. Listen to your customers, staff, other groups in your organization, suppliers, and collaborators, so that you know how you, your team, and its products and services are perceived. Too many managers behave like one-way communication devices; you must learn, both personally and on behalf of your team, to listen.

Avoid a blame culture. Many managers find it difficult to accept that their team is viewed as having a blame culture. It is easier to accept this once you realize that unless you go to extreme lengths to avoid creating a blame culture, by default you will be seen as having created a blame culture. To get an idea of the lengths you must go to, ask yourself the following questions: Are you willing to reward someone who has failed honorably? Are you willing to allow people to have the responsibility for making decisions and then accept the blame from your superiors when things go wrong? Are you willing to genuinely praise people who bring you bad news? Can you give constructive criticism with no blame at all? Once you have answered these questions, ask yourself one more: Are you *still* sure you have not created a blame culture?

Being able to answer yes to this set of questions is really important, because if you want your team members to push their performance to the extremes, to take calculated risks, and to embrace change and other challenges, then you have to avoid creating a blame culture.

Avoid a blame culture.

Avoid an arrogant, insular culture. A common perception of a strong team is that it is insular and arrogant. Unless you are overtly open and conciliatory to your superiors and other teams in your organization, that is how you will be viewed. Make it your job to demonstrate that both you and your team are receptive, communicative, and cooperative—do not be seen as arrogant and insular by default.

Recognize that many of your problems may be in your head. You *can* do most things that you need to do. Recognize that your organization, your customers, your staff, and the Personnel or HR department are not stopping you. If you fail to accomplish your objectives, it is most likely that the obstacle is a mental one. If you have the courage to accept the blame if things go wrong, you will be able to do what you want.

MANAGING DIVERSITY

Sometimes I think that some managers would be happier if all members of their staff were obedient clones. To build good teams, you need a wide pool of staff members with diverse talents upon which to draw. You may need creative people, project managers, writers, presenters, reviewers, analysts, and professional workers; the list is endless. Each different sort of personality and skill-set brings its own specific problems; the better the skill, the more extreme the problems tend to be. Good managers should delight in the diversity and excellence of their staff members, knowing that one of their main jobs is to manage the problems that come with any diverse group of talented people.

Within any group of people, interpersonal tensions may arise. It is important that you show that you respect all the different skills and personalities in your team. In this way, the Golden Rule of Management will help you create a culture in which people respect each other's talents, even if they do not like each other.

BUILDING RELATIONSHIPS

When attempting to build strong, working relationships, you may have to take the lead, initially leaving yourself vulnerable and exposed. As a front-line manager, you may need to give before you can receive, offering trust and respect before people have earned either. The same approach may be needed to establish a solid foundation for honest exchange; often, you will have to behave honestly for an extended period of time before people will treat you with similar openness.

Humility

Of all the characteristics that distinguish the great manager from the merely good one, humility is perhaps the most elusive, and so I conclude this chapter with a warning about the dangers of indulging your own ego.

Although I do not advocate the extreme view that a manager's role is that of a servant of the team, I do encourage you to create an environment in which team members can get on with doing the real work. It may be necessary for you to shield team members from whatever garbage falls from above, to deal with petty bureaucracy, and to make sure that the money keeps rolling in.

A little humility does the front-line manager no harm at all!

SUGGESTED READING

McCormack, Mark H. *What They Still Don't Teach You at Harvard Business School.* New York: Bantam Books, 1990.

A streetwise set of business and management techniques from a highly articulate, self-made businessman. Now somewhat dated, this book considerably influenced how I viewed management when I read it at the start of my management career.

CHAPTER 13

Managing in the Real World

In this book, I have tried to write what paradoxically might be called a theory of practical management, or even a philosophy of practical management. I think it quite likely that my readers will understand the theory I have put forth, but I worry that, when faced with a real-life practical problem, some may find it hard to apply the theory. To give you a chance to think about what you would do in the face of likely problems, this chapter describes nearly two-dozen real-life scenarios and then explains how I might deal with those situations.

WHAT WOULD YOU DO? TWENTY-THREE CHALLENGES

Scenario 1: A member of your team, whom I will call A, complains about sexual harassment by a person I will call B.

An accusation of harassment undoubtedly strikes terror into the heart of every manager, but by initially approaching the problem purely as a fact-gatherer and by suspending judgmental or emotional interpretation, a manager gets started on sorting through to the truth.

When I first learn of an allegation, I ask A to elaborate on the specific complaint but do not offer an opinion or advice until I first have discussed the case with the appropriate HR,

Personnel, and Legal departments, and second, have initiated any necessary investigation. The reason I initially function as a fact-gatherer but do not give an opinion or advice is that, if things turn nasty, my opinions may well be used in evidence against my team, organization, or even against me personally. If I offer any bit of advice, no matter how minor or how sensible it may seem, *what I say as well as what I do not say* may be used in evidence against me.

At the initial meeting, I do the following:

- I find someplace private to meet with A and collect as much information as possible. (Do not be embarrassed about asking specific questions concerning dates, words used, actual physical contact alleged, and so on, because such information is key to documenting the complainant's allegations. In asking specific questions, I do not go into such detail that I might appear to be a voyeur. I record what I am told. I take notes during the meeting and write up the details afterwards. I have the complainant sign and date the record as factual. I may need this record at a later date, and the act of signing the record emphasizes to the complainant the seriousness of making the allegation and of possible actions to come.)
- I assure A that I take harassment complaints very seriously and that I will immediately seek advice from the Personnel or HR department or from legal counsel, as appropriate.
- I ask A whether he or she requires immediate assistance of any kind. I also ask whether he or she can cope with the current situation for a few more days while I set the wheels in motion.

I am very careful to avoid the following:

- While I do express sympathy for the complainant's distress, I do not give any indication that I accept that the complaint is justified. Person B must be regarded as innocent until proven guilty.

- I do not show any signs of skepticism or hostility.
- I neither try to talk the complainant out of filing the complaint, nor try to encourage him or her to make a formal complaint.
- I do not promise to do anything specific until I have had the opportunity to talk to the appropriate set of advisers.
- I avoid all physical contact, vocabulary, or anything that *in any way* might be misinterpreted as inappropriate behavior.

Once I have gathered facts, my next step is to review the company manual for relevant guidance and alert the Personnel, HR, and Legal staffs. I do precisely what the advisers say as anything else can leave me personally exposed.

I will not give additional information about what I do in the case of a harassment complaint because you need to comply with your own organization's processes for handling such complaints. There are, however, three ways in which the front-line manager can help the process.

If possible, find out what the complainant wants done. Determining what the complainant wants done is not as simple as it sounds. Some people will just want the harassment to stop. Others will feel that they are obligated to make a formal complaint to keep the individual from harassing anyone else. The reason for filing the complaint may be that A is seeking retribution and wants to see B punished, or A may feel that he or she deserves some form of compensation. Knowing what A wants can have a material effect on the way the organization handles such a complaint, but organizations often fail to discover this crucial piece of information.

Inform the complainant about the kind of stress that formal filing probably will bring. Many complainants find the process of filing a complaint enormously stressful. As a front-line manager, you have a duty to tell the person what to expect. You cannot ensure that the person can cope with the stress, but you need to provide sufficient information so he or she can decide what strategy to take.

Once the wheels of the formal process have started to roll, it can be very difficult to stop them. I want to be certain that A knows, for example, that changing his or her view of what outcome is wanted or deciding at some later date that I or someone else should confront B with the objective of stopping the alleged harassment may be exceedingly difficult once a complaint has been officially filed.

Ensure that the accused person is also treated fairly. Many organizations unintentionally tend to favor the complainant. In the interest of justice, I make certain that the person being accused is not assumed to be guilty until such time as guilt is proven.

Scenario 2: *You have been brought in to turn around a failing team and you find that the main problem is that a key creative person has left.*

Assuming that I cannot redirect the activities of the team so that the creative role is less important, I take the following steps:

- I confirm that there is no one else on the team who has the potential to step into the departed person's shoes.
- I contact the person who left to find out why he or she left and whether rehiring might be an option. I tell the person that I am now in charge and things are changing. If the individual is not willing to return, I ask whether he or she knows anyone who might be interested in the job.
- If there is no replacement candidate on the team and the departed team member will not agree to return, then I work out how much I can afford to pay a replacement.
- I ask team members to suggest any likely candidates within their network whom they can directly approach about the creative job opportunity.

- I try to offer the job as an opportunity to a young, up-and-coming talent, rather than solely trying to recruit someone who already has an established track record.
- I use advertisements and headhunters when the previous strategies have not been fruitful. I include wording in any advertisement noting that creative ability is as important as a long track record, and I also list a wide salary range, further indicating that I am open-minded about the level of experience required.

Offer an opportunity to a young, up-and-coming talent.

Scenario 3: *A customer is making unreasonable demands on your staff.*

Obviously, you will do everything you can to protect your staff from unreasonable demands, but there will come a time when you will have to decide whether your staff or your customer comes first. However, the cunning manager can usually avoid having to take such a black-or-white stand. I generally use the following approach:

- I talk to the affected staff members and discuss whether there is any way that they can cope with the unreasonable demands. Remember, as I've already noted, I see nothing wrong with the type of bribery in which I offer staff members time off once the job for the customer has been delivered or a bonus or a variety of non-cash inducements.
- I talk to the customer to try to get him or her to behave more reasonably. For example, I might say, "I am worried that the pressure this work is putting my staff under might prejudice the quality of the job we are doing for you. Is there any way we can reduce that pressure?"
- I rotate staff members through the post that deals with the difficult customer.

If you have to make a choice between your staff and that customer, there is no shame in recognizing the power of the customer. An obnoxious but marginal customer makes it much easier to put your staff first. Staff members will realize that they may suffer if a key customer account is lost and so may well accept your backing an important, but difficult, customer.

Scenario 4: *One member of your staff comes to you and says he or she cannot cope with the work load.*

You should be very grateful that the person had the courage to come to tell you about this problem. Many people say nothing, letting themselves, their work, and others on the team all suffer. It is important that you handle this conversation in a way that will encourage other people to do the same.

There are three likely reasons that a person may be unable to perform the work assigned:

- First, the person may have too much to do and, like a deer mesmerized by the oncoming headlights of a car, is frozen in his or her tracks. My solution in such a case is to go through the person's workload with him or her, to discuss the priority of tasks so the person knows whether some items either can be dropped or can be transferred to someone else.
- Second, the person can do most assigned tasks but cannot do one specific part of the job properly. To enable the person to do the full job might necessitate something as simple as providing some specialized training, but it is more likely that the person is doing a job for which he or she has little aptitude. In the latter case, I find it is usually best to assign a change of job.
- Third, the confession by someone about his or her inability to perform the assigned task sometimes may be a cry for help that relates to something other than the person's work. I then look for the real problem and, if necessary, refer the individual to seek professional help.

Scenario 5: *The team faces a critical deadline and people must work extremely long hours in their effort to meet it.*

There are numerous actions I take in this situation:

- Even if I am not working on the pressured project, I make it obvious that I am logging long hours myself. However, I make it clear that I am doing my own work, and that I am not looking over the shoulders of team members.
- I provide a supportive environment, for example by making sure that everyone goes out to eat regularly or by bringing in food for the group myself and eating with the team for that meal. As I've noted previously, the concept of the boss as the servant of the team is a powerful symbol.

- I act as support for and backup to the project manager. With everyone working to capacity, it is very easy for people to lose sight of the forest for the trees. To help people maintain a proper perspective, I periodically gather everyone together to talk about whether the work is being done as efficiently as possible. By contributing an outside perspective, I believe I help team members to spot how extra resources could be redeployed, and to identify hidden risks that are being missed.
- I intervene when people clearly are too tired to work efficiently, sending them out to a meal and a movie or home to sleep—by taxi if necessary.
- I may take command of matters if it is clear the deadline is going to be missed, perhaps by directing the team to deliver less on time or by negotiating a sensible extension.

Scenario 6: *You have a staff member who works incredibly long hours, and refuses to work fewer hours or to slow down.*

Ultimately, it is an individual's right to set his or her own priorities, but if the person's work patterns are resulting in too many mistakes or in antisocial behavior such as extreme rudeness or irritability, then I insist that the person work less hard. Short of forbidding the person to be on the job at certain times, I've gotten my point across by means of a couple of techniques. One technique I occasionally use is to come in to the office after regular hours and send the workaholics home. Or I persuade such people to arrange their schedule to take off specific days each month to spend recreationally or with their families.

Scenario 7: *A major change in office accommodation is about to take place.*

When faced with managing any sort of change to the space people occupy, I reach for a crash helmet. There is almost nothing that arouses stronger passion than changing where—or when, for that matter—people do their work. Many people believe that their physical working environment is critical to both their productivity and quality of life. Add to this the less noble feelings of territory and status, and you have a potentially explosive mixture.

Techniques I have used include the following:

- I find a mother figure or father figure who is liked and respected by the team, and put that person in charge of the change. People tend to behave much better if such a nurturing person is controlling the change. When no such person is available, I take charge and put my full authority behind the decisions.

- I assign less-than-attractive real estate to myself. I learned the value of this technique when I witnessed my manager as he relocated a team from a pod of private offices into open plan. Before assigning people to the new space, he explained he was going into the open plan himself and would not have a window area. By embracing the open plan himself, he kept the full respect of the team.

- I make certain that my reasons for allocating specific accommodations are clearly articulated and rigorously observed. If accommodations are allocated in connection with job requirements, for example, and bear no relationship to status, then I say so and stick to the plan.

- I see to it that team members have plenty of time to get used to the proposed plan, and I make it policy never to spring the allocation on people at the last minute. It takes time for most people to adjust to change, and they are likely to be more receptive to it if they can let the idea simmer awhile.

Never spring the allocation on people at the last minute.

Scenario 8: *A person with a reputation as a long-term under-performer is moved into your team.*

The first action I take when I discover that an under-performer has been assigned to my staff is to ask my contacts in the Personnel or HR departments for advice on how to handle the person. This effort to communicate early about anticipated problems will make it easier if I have to get those departments involved later on.

The second thing I try to do is keep an open mind as I approach the person. It is possible that he or she has been in the wrong job or in the wrong environment, and that, under new leadership, performance will improve.

My tactic is to be very precise in managing the person. Right at the start, I make it clear what I expect of him or her, and I try immediately to set realistic, measurable objectives.

Before I decide what approach to follow, I review the procedures my organization has in place for handling under-performers and ask my contacts in Personnel and HR for advice on how much time the person should have to improve. Sometimes, I decide on a different amount of time from that suggested by my advisers, but I make sure I document my reasons very carefully to preclude accusations of discrimination now or further down the road.

Scenario 9: *A workman comes to you and reports that he possibly has drilled into asbestos.*

There are some situations in which one cannot afford to take chances; on the top of my list are issues involving my staff's health and safety. Unless I know unequivocally that a workman could not have drilled into asbestos or that a colleague is mistaken who reports that a deranged gunman is roaming the halls, I would immediately clear and seal off the affected area at the first indication of such a serious health or safety crisis. If the event seems both criminal and life-threatening, I would alert internal security, my management, and, if appropriate, the police. Because I have always worked in large government and corporate settings, I've had a Health and Safety department and a Security department to notify, but common sense should tell you what to do in your own environment. If I could not get an instant response from whatever internal department my policy required me to notify, I would immediately escalate the issue within the appropriate department, and if this did not yield quick results, then escalate it up the management chain.

Scenario 10: *You suspect that one of your staff members is taking kickbacks from a supplier.*

One of the things every front-line manager needs to understand is when to act on his or her own responsibility and when to call in the "experts." Suspicion of criminal activity, such as a team member accepting kickbacks from a vendor, is one of the cases in which I would hotfoot it to my Personnel or HR department, to Security, to Legal, or directly to the police. One rule of thumb is that anything that could possibly end up in court should go straight to the experts, whose advice I recommend following to the letter.

Scenario 11: *The person on your team you are using as your internal personnel officer resigns or is transferred to another job.*

Anyone with knowledge of internal personnel matters and the skill to handle them is a key employee, whether he or she serves only your team or the entire organization. When I lose such a key employee, I know I have a problem because the loss usually means that I must assume the role myself. The reason I do this is that I believe it is best to leave such a sensitive position vacant until a truly qualified replacement can be found. Generally, I have not had a team member waiting in the wings who could immediately step into the vacated position, but if there is an obvious replacement, then this scenario is a no-brainer. The problem comes when there is no obvious replacement. I usually find that it is best to leave the position vacant, but it takes some confidence to leave an intractable problem alone "until something turns up." However, that is often better than making a bad decision.

Scenario 12: *An exceedingly important project has hit major problems.*

When a critical or highly visible project hits the wall, the first question a front-line manager should ask is whether the project manager needs assistance. If the project manager is one of my top people, then I ask what help is needed, and take action based on the answer. If the troubled project is led by a marginally qualified manager, I usually take the lead in deciding the strategy for sorting out the problems.

It is important to ensure that appropriately vigorous measures have been taken. As I have noted previously, it is easy to underestimate how hard and fast a front-line manager may need to react to a problem.

I also take a high-profile role in handling the customers who are affected by the problem. I often discover that the team is more focused on solving the problem than on addressing the effects that the problem has on customers.

Ensure that appropriately vigorous measures have been taken.

Scenario 13: *One of your key staff members is rubbing other team members the wrong way.*

When I have a staff member whose behavior and attitude irritate other members of the team, I do the obvious: I explain to both sides how the other side perceives them. In certain cases, I find it effective to be visibly annoyed with both sides. Statements such as "I don't care who's right and who's wrong" or "I don't expect everyone to be friends, but I do expect you all to act like professionals" can help to defuse emotions and make both parties behave better.

Some level of tension within a team is normal, and it is seldom possible to remove all such tensions. A front-line manager must learn to manage them when they cannot be removed.

Scenario 14: *You are told by your management to brief your staff with information that you think is probably untrue.*

This scenario is troubling to me for two reasons. First, a practical reason: Because I do not know what a front-line manager in this situation really should do, I am reluctant to share what I myself have done. Second, a moral reason: Because I suspect that there is no right answer, I also suspect there is no good answer.

When I moved from being a research scientist to the position of manager of research scientists and information systems professionals, one of the things that struck me was that it was much easier to know whether I was doing a good job as a research scientist than it was as a manager. As a researcher, I could usually measure in some way how good my work was. The same is not true of management. The world of the manager is often not black and white; it is various shades of gray. In this particular scenario, the shades are dark gray, much closer to the side of evil than to the side of good. If you toe the party line and convey information you believe to be untrue, then you jeopardize your own integrity and reputation. If you admit your doubts, then your organization will correctly accuse you of a lack of loyalty. Heads they win, tails you lose.

The reader is entitled to know what I would do—and actually have done—in this situation. So here goes: I give the briefing as provided to me. Then, I say that I suspect there is more to the matter than meets the eye, and state that I further suspect that we will only find out the full picture in time.

Scenario 15: *You have a brilliant idea to develop a new business opportunity, but know that if you tell your managers about it, they will place so many obstacles in your way that it will probably never happen.*

I may be about to surprise you, but I know where the corporate obstructionists are coming from. Unfortunately, to fully explain all the issues involved in developing a new business opportunity, I would need a chapter in an entirely different book. It is possible, however, for me to raise just a few of the questions and issues that are frequently overlooked in developing a new business opportunity.

Is the opportunity scaleable? I have a colleague who calls this problem of scale the "problem of success." The growth in demand for a service is seldom uniform. If a business opportunity is a success, then success usually happens in a short period of time with demand suddenly increasing dramatically. In this situation, I ask myself whether my team, or my organization, can handle such explosive growth in terms of staff, facilities, and so on. My organization needs to decide if we can handle the problems of success.

What is the worst financial scenario that could happen? Very few managers appreciate the importance of analyzing the worst possible scenario if a business opportunity fails to succeed. Questions my organization should ask me include the following: How much will it cost to manage the small existing customer base of a product or service if the organization ceases to offer that product or service? How much damage to existing products and brands could failure inflict? Could the organization end up being sued? This last question is a fine example of why my organization does need to examine potential business opportunities.

Can I protect the opportunity from "fast followers"? It is often mistakenly thought that being the first to market is one of the keys to business success. It is a myth because it is the first organization to create what the market regards as a leading *brand* for the product or service that often makes the most money. It is not uncommon for one organization to prove that there is a market for a new product or service, only to have its early lead overtaken by a so-called fast follower who has an existing brand to leverage or the resources and infrastructure to rapidly build volume sales and a strong new brand. Many managers do not understand the issues relating to developing a brand and will need to depend on experts within their organization.

I could go on and on about all the pitfalls of which a manager may not be aware when developing a new business opportunity. I wish I could reassure you that all the hoops that your organization will make you jump through are really necessary—producing entirely fictional revenue projections is a personal pet peeve—but there are usually a lot of sound reasons why your organization will demand to review your plans.

One technique that is worth thinking about is whether you can hide the start of the development of a new business opportunity. It is often possible to find space in your budget to do a bit of speculative development. Because this hidden development can be considered a kind of research (and presumably a good thing), it can sometimes increase the chances of getting corporate approval for a new opportunity, especially if you can demonstrate some level of prototype. An additional advantage of this approach is that many business opportunities will fail at the earliest stages and it can be useful to weed out the obvious duds before raising the visibility of an opportunity outside of your team.

Scenario 16: *You have a project manager on your team who has a very laid-back approach to project management and does not seem to worry as much as you would about delivering projects on time and within budget. The particular manager has run a number of projects, which despite your worries have come in within budget and on time. Do you deploy this person on a very important, high visibility project, and, if so, do you institute any additional controls?*

I have encountered this situation on a number of occasions. In a previous chapter, I noted that when you delegate a task, you also delegate the ability to do that task differently from the way you would have done it yourself. When I noted this, I had in mind the fact that the plan chosen to achieve the objective might well be substantially different from the plan you would have created. I think the same principle extends to other areas in which delegated authority is exercised in a different way from what you originally had in mind. I also think that people have a right to be judged by their results, and if this project manager has a record of delivering, then he or she is entitled to your trust. Having said that, I must confess that I usually have been very diligent in reviewing progress with such people to ensure that I do not lose sleep on their behalf.

Scenario 17: *A, a member of your staff you trust, comes and tells you that B, another member of your team, has approached A about joining a new company B is thinking of starting.*

My view is that you are entitled to be completely ruthless with anyone within your team trying to poach all, or part, of your team. In such a "he said, she said" situation, however, I would check with my Personnel or HR department to ensure first that the company will back me if I initiate a discussion with the poacher regarding the accusation, and second, that the company will back me in instantly dismissing the person doing the poaching, if it is confirmed. Because all companies and all legislative jurisdictions have specific sets of laws protecting workers from unfair dismissal, you will need to discuss with your own management, Personnel, HR, and Legal departments whether they need more evidence before you confront the potential poacher.

In such a situation, I also assess what assurances the potential poacher could give that would restore sufficient trust for me to keep him or her on staff. If you face this situation, it is worthwhile to confirm with Personnel or HR what your organization's policy is.

When I confront the person, I always try to have a representative from Personnel or HR present. I listen carefully to any explanation that the accused person offers to determine whether there is substantial possibility that he or she is not guilty of gross disloyalty. In the event that the evidence is sufficiently clear, then the accused person should be dismissed. In Chapter 2, in which I discussed termination, I stated procedures for dismissal, so I will only reiterate here that the dismissed individual must turn over all passes, keys, computer access, and so on, before leaving the site.

Assuming that the accusation is accurate, that there is no possibility of keeping the potential poacher on staff, and that dismissal is inevitable, I always have legal counsel present at the dismissal to warn about legal actions that will be instigated against the start-up company if it makes unlawful use of confidential information from my organization. In truth, the chances of winning such actions are small, but awareness of the costs, in time and money, of defending such an action can cause some start-ups to think twice before using proprietary information.

Once dismissal has been finalized, I try to minimize any damage the dismissed person might do to my organization. One advantage of quick-and-ruthless treatment is that the person will probably take some time to get his or her start-up company running, so I have a breathing space during which I can take action to limit or control the problems the start-up can cause. Some steps I take follow:

- I notify all staff of the dismissal and explain the reasons for it, alerting staff members to the possibility that the dismissed person may well try to contact them—both to poach them and to make mischief.
- I determine whether there are underlying causes of discontent among the staff that would make it easier for a poacher to operate, and move quickly to address any solvable problems.
- I approach any customers with whom the dismissed staff member had contact, and explain why the person's employment was terminated—I get advice from my legal counsel as to what and how much I can say before I raise the subject with customers because I don't want to provide a basis for a lawsuit brought by my former employee. It is important to make sure that the customers are happy with your plans to move forward with them now that the person has left.

Scenario 18: *You go to get yourself a coffee and find a group of your team members joking about an incident that seriously breaks health and safety rules.*

As a general rule, I think that managers should not lose their temper. I also think that a manager should only criticize staff in private. But there are times when the general rules do not apply. Personally, I have been known to do a passable impression of a Titan rocket lifting off the pad when I have come upon a situation in which jokes are being made about a safety or health infraction. I do not tolerate my team acting in such a way, and I do not recommend that anyone else tolerate such behavior.

Scenario 19: *You come across a situation in which it is pretty clear that one member of your team is bullying another member of your team.*

In the situation in which one team member bullies another, I have no patience and am tempted to publicly tear a strip off the bully. It is better, however, to take the bully to a private office to warn him or her that such behavior will not be tolerated. Although I do not worry if it is pretty obvious from my body language that I am furious as I march the bully off for the dressing down, the reprimand is better done in private. My objective is to stop the bullying but not to cause public humiliation.

If the scenario were one in which I overheard not bullying, but rather a racist or sexist joke, I would tear the strip off the joke-teller in public. Telling such jokes shows an appalling lack of judgment, but my reason for dressing down the teller in public is that I want the message of humiliation to be communicated to all who might overhear my fury. I make it clear that this behavior must be stopped. If anyone who overhears the dressing down has told such jokes, he or she also will get my message, and will possibly think, "There, but for the grace of God, go I."

Scenario 20: *Your boss asks you to do something that you think is in your boss's best interest but will harm your organization.*

There is no simple way to handle this dilemma, so what I will try to do is dissect the possible responses I might make, and analyze the reasons why I choose one or another of the various responses.

There seem to me to be four possible responses, in varying degrees of forcefulness:

1. I do as asked without protest.
2. I tell my boss I am uncomfortable with the request and try to engage him or her in a discussion that I hope will lead to withdrawal of the request.
3. I refuse the request, saying politely why I cannot carry it out.
4. I ask my boss's boss, or someone else in authority, what I should do.

How should you choose your response? Unfortunately, this is one of those situations that is unlikely to be black or white; it will most likely be an infuriating shade of gray.

One key factor I consider is the seriousness of the damage I might do to my organization if I carry out my boss's orders. If the damage would be minor, then a less extreme action such as option 1 or 2 can be justified; but if the damage would be major, or the request is immoral or illegal, then option 3 or 4 is my probable response. A question I ask myself is, "If my boss's boss finds out, how angry would he or she be that I did not report the situation?"

The second major factor is the personality of my boss. If he or she is an autocratic person likely to bear a grudge, then I believe I would be better off going for either a weak action (option 1) or a very strong response (option 4). If the boss is usually fairly reasonable, then an option-2 response might well be appropriate. If the boss is fairly weak and cowardly, then option 2 or 3 could work.

I cannot offer more definitive advice here, but this scenario shows that there will be times when you will find yourself in a no-win situation, in which you have to make a choice from a number of seemingly unappealing options.

Scenario 21: *You decide that what you are being asked to do is so serious that you tell your boss's boss, who doesn't want to know and says you must make your own decision.*

If I raise a problem formally with my organization and find that my organization does not take responsibility in any way, then I view myself as having discharged my responsibilities to the organization. Further pursuit of the matter or further escalation can quickly give me a reputation as a troublemaker and can easily damage my career. In such a case, I do make the decision myself as to what to do, but I create a written record of the matter and any conversations.

The decision I make would be either to carry out the instructions of the boss or to refuse to carry out the instructions—there remain no other practical choices. If the issue is solely one of damage to the organization, I ask that the instruction be put in writing. Then I would probably just do it. If I were being asked to do something immoral or illegal, I would refuse to do it and politely explain why I believe the action to be immoral or illegal. Were my boss to continue to insist, then I would ask that the instruction be put in writing, answer the request by putting my refusal in writing, and then send the whole to my boss with a copy to my boss's boss. Taking this action will make life very difficult for future dealings with the boss, but there are times when principles must be lived up to—and this is one of them.

Scenario 22: *Your new boss is a micromanager who keeps getting unnecessarily involved in the details of your team's tasks.*

Telling your boss to butt out is tempting but I have not found it to be the answer. Taking this approach is highly risky, and even if the boss takes the message without shooting you, he or she is unlikely to stop micromanaging. I try to develop a relationship with the boss that will allow me to discuss what I consider to be micromanagement. Failing that, or until my relationship has developed sufficiently that the boss does butt out, I attempt to make the best of the situation, and try to avoid getting stressed out by something I cannot change.

There are, however, a couple of things I do to mitigate the damage. First, I try to ensure that all the financial aspects of the team and all issues that impact the bottom line are kept in perfect order. This is one of the best ways to reassure a micromanager, and provides protection if he or she starts to criticize me; someone who is delivering according to budget seldom gets punished.

Second, I make sure I give my boss a monthly, written progress report. This will provide both reassurance and the protection of showing that I have noted areas of risk in advance of their occurrence.

Your boss is a micromanager who keeps getting unnecessarily involved in details.

Scenario 23: *Your new boss blames you, rather than backs you up, when things go wrong.*

My strategy is virtually identical to that given for the last scenario, with one addition:

I try to be very conservative in my budgeting, because my blaming boss probably will not back me up if I fail to meet an ambitious target. I also try not to over-deliver, because a blaming boss may well inflate next year's targets if I do. It is fairly easy to push revenue from one year into the next, to bring myself closer to budget, knowing I can then offer a higher budget target next year, because I am already partway to meeting it.

Usually with a blaming boss, I try to adopt a similarly conservative approach to deadlines and targets that come up during the year.

SUMMARY

I did not find this an easy chapter to write: In fact, I think I found this the most challenging chapter of them all. In this chapter, I am far from sure that the advice I am offering on the practice of management is anything like "best practice." I do, however, think that this chapter shows that real-world management decisions are *hard*.

Yesterday, I had to reprimand one of my staff for a minor issue of misconduct. An hour after my conversation, I was still physically shaking. I must have had hundreds of similar conversations, indeed many more serious conversations, over the past ten years, and here I was still having a noticeable physical reaction. My point: Even experienced managers can find it very unpleasant to face difficult issues.

I do recommend that you, as a front-line manager, try to develop a support network with whom you can discuss difficult issues. Cultivate your advisers in the Personnel or HR department, and any other advisers your organization has available. Try to develop a relationship with some of your most senior and experienced staff, so that you can talk difficult problems through with them. Ultimately, you must shoulder the burden of making the hard decisions, and there are times when you must react instantly, but you will find that having a number of trusted lieutenants can be a great support to you.

CHAPTER 14

Drawing Conclusions

One of my friends who read an early draft of this book shocked me by saying that he believed that what I had written was a book about my philosophy of management. At first, his interpretation greatly bothered me because I feel that the word *philosophy* sounds pretentious, but I think he may have been on to something. This book does describe the practice as well as the art and science of front-line management, but it does also reflect my philosophy. In concluding this book, I find that I want to make some overtly philosophical points.

A PHILOSOPHY OF MANAGEMENT

We are used to regarding certain professions as reflecting a calling that goes well beyond the desire to earn a living—for example, most ministers, medical practitioners, soldiers, and teachers seem not to be motivated by mundane issues like money but rather are driven by a profound desire to help others. People who enter such professions touch the lives of the people they serve. Although few people would regard management as a noble endeavor, the way managers touch people's lives makes our jobs very significant to society. A good manager can enhance both the lives of the people he or she manages and the people the team interacts with. Truly great managers also should have many of the qualities associated with the overtly noble professions, such as courage and integrity.

Management as a noble endeavor.

Many managers do regard money as a motivator, but most are more concerned about the way money can provide secure employment for team members than about its role in a reward system. If not money, what really motivates managers?

Ambition

Anyone seeking to move up in a career must have ambition. I see ambition as a complex emotion with three important parts. I have coined a phrase—"the three faces of ambition"—to describe the things that motivate people when they are actively seeking career advancement. The first motivator is the recognition, status, and money a person gets from filling a management position well. The second is the enjoyment a person may get from exercising power over others. The third is the pleasure one feels when making things happen. Even if it is the third face of ambition alone that is your main motivation, it is quite likely that you will get a buzz from the first two, which are, however, a bit like recreational drugs—you can find yourself becoming addicted to them. Recognizing the risks of the first two faces of ambition is the first step to ensuring that you can cope with them. People who are driven by one or both of the first two faces of ambition—without the third—are generally a danger to themselves and others.

For an ambitious person, the disappointment of being a failure at whatever goals he or she sets can be as stressful as actually making it to the top! Ambitious people should decide what price they are willing to pay to realize their ambitions.

The porch-swing test

I devised the *porch-swing test* to help people think about what they should do with their life and career. To take the test, imagine that you are eighty years old and you are sitting on your porch swing just after being told that you have a terminal illness. Okay, this situation is grim to imagine, . . . but bear with me: Look back and think about the decisions you have made during your life and career. Are you happy with those decisions? If your answer is no, now think about what you could change that will help assure that you will look back proudly when you eventually are an octogenarian.

It is my view that you should think about what you really value in your life. What will give you fulfillment? You need to think about the balance between the fulfillment you can get from your work and the fulfillment you get from your family, from learning new things, from your outside interests, and from what you can put back into society.

CONCENTRATE ON THE JOB, NOT THE TITLE

I did not follow a career plan that predicted what was to come. True, I had a fuzzy notion of what I hoped for, but work and life take one along strange roads, and my career has been no exception. It is probable that in any career a person will encounter many opportunities, but the lucky person is the one who seizes the right opportunities. I chose the challenges that excited me, most frequently because the job on offer could help me achieve something I felt was really worthwhile and something I would be proud to achieve.

An invaluable lesson I learned quite early on was not to be too scared of making a mistake. A career is a bit like driving a car; if you take a wrong turn, you can always reverse gear and back out.

My approach has worked for me. I encourage you to find an approach that will work for you.

THE BEST JOB IN THE WORLD

Throughout this book, I have tried to highlight the difficult challenges a person must face in a drive to become a great manager, but now I will concentrate on the positive aspects of being a manager. It is a great job, but why do I think it is so great?

For me, there are three amazingly satisfying experiences associated with management. The first is the experience of having a vision of where the team should go and seeing the team embracing and then realizing that vision. Second, there is the pleasure that comes from helping your people to develop their potential and to overcome the problems that they face. Third, there is the feeling of achievement when you experience the emergence of a team identity of which team members are proud to be part. People who belong to a team with a great culture will carry that memory with them for the rest of their careers; those who go into management may well be inspired to create great teams of their own.

I have seen little research that indicates how much difference a good manager can make to a team. My observation is that a well-managed team performs significantly better than a less well-led team. Indeed, the difference can be as stark as the difference between life and death for the team. If you are a good manager, you almost certainly earn your salary, and then some.

LAST WORDS

I hope that some of what I have written has struck a chord with you. You cannot learn management from a book, but you can gain a better understanding of why some things work, and why other things are almost guaranteed to fail. I encourage you to practice your art and to constantly try out new ideas to see if they work for you.

Index

project management, 120–21
security, 119
staff, *xviii*, 115ff., 136, 137, 187
Infrastructure, 168, 186–87, 244
Initiatives, *xviii*, 7, 199–200, 202
Integrity, 70–72, 221–22
developing, 71
faking, 71, 221
straight-bat approach, 222
Interest, 9, 10, 144, 145–46, 169
feigning, 9
healthy, 10
Interruptions, 8, 9

Job performance, 3–4, 7, 13, 15–16, 18, 19, 27, 32, 38, 44, 52, 53, 58, 60, 82, 149, 154, 176, 189, 201, 214, 223, 227, 239
menial, 89, 181
Jokes in the workplace, 54, 57, 151, 218, 248
Judgment, 20, 28, 70, 72–73, 74, 99, 108, 160, 194, 224, 248

Key staff, 27, 33–38, 158, 172, 242
Knowledge, 105, 112, 127, 135, 199, 241
Knowledge of context, 75

Law, 46, 112, 113–14
Lawyers, *xvi*, 113–15, 136
Leader, *xvii*, *xviii*, 4, 61–79, 81–82, 221. *See also* Leadership; Manager.
authoritarian, 62–63
qualities of, *xvii*, 60, 64–79
vision and. *See* Vision.
young, 81–82
Leadership
courage and, 73–74

defined, 60–61
determination and, 72
do's and don'ts of, 89–93
honesty and, 70
myths, 61–64
opportunities for, 86–88
passion and, 69–70
practice of, 80–94
principles of, *xvii*, 59–79
project management and, 98, 99
responsibility and, 74
roles, 82–86
style, 80–82, 94
team, *xv–xvi*, 59–79, 80–94, 98, 99
Legal issues, 38, 45, 113–14, 216–17, 246
Lister, Timothy, 18n., 152
Literal-Reading Warning, *xix–xx*, 75
Logbook, 175

Management. *See also* Golden Rule; Leader; Manager; Team.
as noble endeavor, 253–54
do's and don'ts, 23–32
manipulation and, 5, 6, 12
parenting and, 3–4, 6, 32
philosophy of, 253–55
practice of, *xix*
principles of, 3–4, 32
processes, 145
scenarios, 230–52
theory of, *xix*, *xvi–xvii*
turnaround. *See* Turnaround management.
Management by Objectives, 169
Management paradox, 27, 63–64
Management-speak, 30, 169
Manager, 4, 13–23, 222ff., 254–55.